THE TOMB CHAMBER OF *Ḥsw* THE ELDER
PART 1: ILLUSTRATIONS

AMERICAN RESEARCH CENTER IN EGYPT REPORTS

Volume 10

The Tomb Chamber of *Ḥsw* the Elder:
The Inscribed Material at Kom el-Hisn

Part 1: Illustrations

Other publications in this series:

1. *Quseir al-Qadim 1978: Preliminary Report,* by D. S. Whitcomb and J. H. Johnson
2. *Mendes I.* by R. K. Holz, D. Stieglitz, D. P. Hansen, and E. Ochsenschlager
4. *Cities of the Delta, Part I: Naukratis: Preliminary Report on the 1977–78 and 1980 Seasons,* by W. D. E. Coulson, A. Leonard, Jr.
5. *Cities of the Delta, Part II: Mendes: Preliminary Report on the 1979 and 1980 Seasons,* by K. L. Wilson
6. *Cities of the Delta, Part III: Tell el-Maskhuṭa: Preliminary Report on the Wadi Tumilat Project 1978–1979,* by J. S. Holladay, Jr.
7. *Quseir al-Qadim 1980: Preliminary Report,* by D. S. Whitcomb and J. H. Johnson
8. *Fusṭāṭ Expedition Final Report, vol. 1: Catalogue of Filters.* by G. T. Scanlon
9. *Archaeological Investigations at el-Hibeh 1980: Preliminary Report,* by R. J. Wenke
11. *Fusṭāṭ Expedition Final Report, vol. 2: Fusṭāṭ-C,* by W. Kubiak and G. T. Scanlon

THE TOMB CHAMBER
OF *Ḥsw* THE ELDER:
The Inscribed Material at Kom El-Ḥisn
Part 1: Illustrations

by

David P. Silverman

Published for

THE AMERICAN RESEARCH CENTER IN EGYPT, INC.

by

EISENBRAUNS

WINONA LAKE

1988

Excavations at Naukratis conducted under the sponsorship of the National Endowment for the Humanities.

Publications of the Ancient Naukratis Project

William D. E. Coulson
Albert Leonard, Jr.
Co-directors

Vol. 3. The Tomb Chamber of *Ḥsw* the Elder, Part 1: Illustrations, by David P. Silverman (ARCE/Reports, vol. 10)
Vol. 6. Greek Painted Pottery from Naukratis in Egyptian Museums, by Marjorie Susan Venit (ARCE/Catalogs, vol. 7)

Produced for the American Research Center in Egypt
and distributed by

Eisenbrauns
POB 275
Winona Lake, Indiana 46580

Library of Congress Cataloging in Publication Data

Silverman, David P.
   The tomb chamber of Hsw the Elder: the inscribed material at
Kom-el-Hisn / by David P. Silverman.
   p.   cm. — (American Research Center in Egypt reports; v. 10–)

Includes bibliographical references.
Contents: pt. 1. Illustrations.
1. Hisn, Kawm al- (Egypt) 2. Hsw, The Elder—Tomb.
3. Tombs—Egypt. 4. Egypt—Antiquities.
I. American Research Center in Egypt.
II. Title. III. Series.
DT73.H57S56 1988
932—dc19   88-21278
ISBN 0-936770-17-1   CIP

CONTENTS

FOREWORD

THE NAUKRATIS PROJECT

The Naukratis Project has consisted of work in the western Nile Delta, specifically in an area bounded by the sites of El-Barnugi in the north and Kom el-Ḥisn in the south.[1] This area contains the ancient city of Naukratis (Kom Geʾif) (Fig. 1), which according to the Greek historian Herodotus, was the first and only city in which the early Greek merchants were allowed to settle. The area also contains other sites of occupation from Pharaonic through late Roman times. Unfortunately, little is known of these sites and their state of preservation. Indeed, the process of decay and modern encroachment is so serious in the Delta that a resolution was passed at the Second International Congress of Egyptologists held at Grenoble, France, in September, 1979, giving priority to survey work in the Delta. The situation is particularly serious in the western Delta where, in the Behera Province alone, there are some 180 sites whose existence is threatened by both natural and human agents. Accordingly, the Naukratis Project has involved: 1) a program of excavation at Naukratis based on modern techniques and backed by an interdisciplinary support staff. Preliminary results of these excavations have been published elsewhere[2] together with a detailed account of the Project's scope and aims; 2) a survey of all ancient sites within an approximate 30 km. area to the north and west of Naukratis (Fig. 1) in order to learn more about the environs of the city. Such a survey has assessed the character of the visible remains, the state of site preservation, and the extent of intrusions made by modern settlements and cultivation.

Part of the survey work was concentrated at Kom el-Ḥisn, a site that appears to have been occupied continuously from at least the Old Kingdom through late Roman times.

[1] The Naukratis Project was funded by matching grants from the National Endowment for the Humanities, and the authors wish to acknowledge the Endowment's support. Matching funds were provided by the Graduate School and the College of Liberal Arts at the University of Minnesota, by the Social Sciences and Humanities Research Council of Canada, by the University of Missouri at Columbia, Carleton College, the College of St. Catherine, Gustavus Adolphus College, Honeywell, Inc., the 3H Industries in Sunnyvale, California, and by private individuals. The co-directors of the project are William Coulson, University of Minnesota, and Albert Leonard, Jr., University of Missouri-Columbia. The authors wish to acknowledge the invaluable help provided by the American Research Center in Egypt, especially its executive director, Paul Walker, and its Cairo director, Robert Wenke.

[2] W. D. E. Coulson and A. Leonard, Jr., "A Preliminary Survey of the Naukratis Region in the Western Nile Delta," *JFA* 6 (1979) 151–68; *Cities of the Delta I, Naukratis* (Malibu 1981); "Investigations at Naukratis and Environs, 1980 and 1981," *AJA* 86 (1982) 361–80; W. D. E. Coulson, A. Leonard, Jr., and N. C. Wilkie, "Three Seasons of Excavations and Survey at Naukratis and Environs," *JARCE* 20, in press.

Preliminary reports of the survey[3] and epigraphic[4] work accomplished at Kom el-Hisn have already been published and this volume now contains the final publication of the inscribed material there.

William D. E. Coulson
Albert Leonard, Jr.
Co-Directors, Naukratis Project

[3] W. D. E. Coulson and A. Leonard, Jr., *JFA* (in note 2) 163–67; *Naukratis* (in note 2) 81–85.
[4] D. P. Silverman, "Epigraphic Work at Kom el-Hisn, 1981," *NARCE* 116 (Winter 1981–82) 6–11.

PREFACE

The Epigraphic Survey is a part of the Naukratis Expedition, organized and co-directed by William Coulson of the University of Minnesota and Albert Leonard, Jr. of the University of Missouri. It is through their efforts that information from this important area in the Delta is being brought to light. However, the work of the Survey could not have been done without the generous support and concern of the Egyptian Antiquities Organization. Both the office in Cairo and the local inspectorate encouraged and advised the Expedition during the field seasons. The former Directors of the American Research Center in Egypt, Paul Walker in New York and James Allen in Cairo, were instrumental in expediting our activities, and the Center sponsored our project. Moreover, Dr. Allen graciously deferred his interests in publishing the inscriptions in the tomb to the Survey.

The major epigraphic work occurred during the months of May, June, and July of 1981 under the direction of David P. Silverman and the expert assistance of Roberta Dougherty and David Pendlebury, all of the University of Pennsylvania. Support for the activities of the Survey came from a matching grant from the National Endowment for the Humanities. A preliminary season took place during the summer months of 1980 with Silverman in overall charge and field work carried out by Paul Brodie of the University of Pennsylvania and Margaret Serpico of Brandeis University. Photographic records were made by the Expedition photographer, Duane Bingham.

The publication of the results of the field work has been the responsibility of David Silverman, with various parts being carefully prepared by Roberta Dougherty, Sophia Kelly, and David Pendlebury. The University Museum and the Research Foundation of the University of Pennsylvania has generously aided in the preparation of the material for publication, and the work has greatly benefitted from the support of the Work-Study Program of the University of Pennsylvania and a grant from the Translations Program of the Division of Research Programs of the National Endowment for the Humanities. The American Research Center has undertaken the financial responsibility of publishing the epigraphic work of the Survey.

The material recorded in the following pages is the result of a large collaborative effort, on both an institutional and individual level. This volume could not have been completed without the considerable effort of many people over the course of the last four years. It is their dedication that has made the publication of the Epigraphic Survey of the Naukratis Expedition possible.

David P. Silverman
December 1984

INTRODUCTION

Although a comparatively well-preserved monument in the Delta, the tomb of *Ḥsw* has received little attention since its discovery by C. C. Edgar in 1910.[1] Only the limestone chamber remains today; there no longer are traces of the mud-brick walls, recorded by Edgar, that may have been the remnants of an adjacent room. Edgar's report was clearly meant to be preliminary, but he adequately described the major features of the monument and presented a reasonable picture of the decorated surfaces of the tomb and some of the inscriptions. Facsimile drawings of the reliefs and inscriptions were apparently never made, and the funerary texts copied by Lacau were never published.

The present volume is devoted to documenting reliefs and the inscriptions in the tomb of *Ḥsw*, the Elder, the largest and most significant monument studied by the Epigraphic Survey. It contains facsimile drawings of the reliefs and large hieroglyphic inscriptions carved in sunk relief on the interior and exterior surfaces. There were areas where the condition of the interior walls precluded tracing: on the South wall and the lower portions of the East and West walls. Parts of the ceiling also were inaccessible. However, those areas that contained inscriptions, but could not be traced, were copied by hand, and they are presented in standardized hieroglyphs in the order, orientation, and proportions that they had in their original position.[2] The volume also includes photographs of the tomb made during the recent survey, as well as photographs, reproduced here though the kindness of the Oriental Institute, that document the lower parts of the interior walls earlier in the century.

The figures in the book have been organized in an attempt to present as complete a picture of the tomb chamber and its reliefs and inscriptions as possible. Toward this end there is a detailed outline of all of the illustrations utilized. Two epigraphers in the field, Dougherty and Pendlebury, have contributed to the preparation of the material in this volume: Roberta Dougherty has meticulously inked in all of the facsimile drawings, and David Pendlebury has provided the hand copy of and other information about the menu of funerary offerings on the East wall. All of the material collected in the field has been collated again, in Philadelphia, and each of the eight hundred and fifteen lines of funerary texts redrawn. The final versions of these texts and the menu were recopied in careful detail by Sophia Kelly, and she and Ms. Dougherty assisted in the coordination of material for the manuscript; Melissa Robinson has contributed her invaluable editorial assistance.

In order to expedite the publication of the tomb of *Ḥsw*, the material has been divided into two parts, the first part devoted to the documentation of the reliefs and inscriptions on

---

[1] For a list of the sources referring to the tomb, see D. Silverman, "Epigraphic Work at Kom el Ḥisn, 1981," *American Research Center in Egypt Newsletter*, 116, Winter 1981/82, p. 10, note 5, and W. Helck, and E. Otto, *Lexikon der Ägyptologie*, Bd. III, (Wiesbaden: Otto Harrassowitz, 1979), p.673–674.

[2] All of the hand copies are divided into columns as are the original texts; the vertical lines used for separation in the copies are not, however, always present on the walls.

the walls of the tomb and the second part of this work, now in preparation, devoted to the analysis of this information: the translation of and commentary on all of the inscriptions in the tomb, a section examining orthographic and paleographic peculiarities, and an index of words used in the texts. There will also be an appendix of other inscriptions, mostly dating to the Ramesside Period and later, that were copied by the Survey at the site of Kom el-Ḥisn and areas nearby.[3] The two parts of the volume, however, are not meant to be an exhaustive study of this monument. The goal of the Epigraphic Survey was to record and analyze the inscribed material at the site, and the present and proposed volume together will attempt to provide that information. Clearly, the tomb and its environment should be subjected to careful archaeological analysis for a total picture.[4]

---

[3] Silverman, "Epigraphic Work," p. 6, and notes 1–4. See also W. Coulson and A. Leonard, Jr. *Cities of the Delta, Part I, Naukratis* (Malibu:, Undena Publications, 1981), pp. 81–85.

[4] *Ibid.*

OUTLINE FOR ILLUSTRATIONS IN
THE TOMB CHAMBER OF *ḤSW* THE ELDER

		Figure	**Reference***
I	**The Site of Kom el-Ḥisn**		
	A. Maps of the Area	1a	photo W.C.
		1b	photo R.W.
	B. View of the Area, looking South	2	slide R.L.D. 1
	C. Plan of the Tomb	3	drawing 21
	D. View of the Tomb, inside protective	4	
	housing, looking North		slide D.P.S. 1
II	**The Tomb Chamber of *Ḥsw*, the Elder, Exterior**		
	A. View, looking North	5	slide 27
	B. Northern Façade[1]		
	1. Overall View	6a	slide D.P.S. 2
	a. diagram	6b	drawing 25a
	2. Composite Drawing	7	drawings 1–5
	3. Lintel		
	a. photograph	8a–g	slides 18–24
	b. drawing	9	drawing 1
	4. Left Jamb (East)		
	a. photograph	10a–i	slides 1–9
	b. drawing	11a–b	drawings 2–3
	5. Right Jamb (West)		
	a. photograph	12a–h	slides 10–17
	b. drawing	13a–b	drawings 4–5
III	**The Tomb Chamber of *Ḥsw*, the Elder, Interior[2]**		
	A. South Wall		
	1. Overall View		

---

* Reference is the term for the source of the illustration presented on the plate; drawing refers to the facsimiles made in the field, and slide refers to the 35mm transparencies taken at the site (if there are no initials listed, the photographer was Bingham; R.L.D. refers to Dougherty, and D.P.S. refers to Silverman). Photo refers to an original photograph reproduced here through permission of the owner (R.W. refers to Robert Wenke, W.C. stands for Coulson, and OI stands for the Oriental Institute of the University of Chicago.

[1] The northern façade is the only exterior surface to be decorated.

[2] The South, West, and East walls were decorated; the North wall was carved only on the exterior surface. The order in which the walls are presented here reflects the numeration originally given to the funerary texts; see L. Lesko, *Index of the Spells*

	Figure	**Reference**
a. diagram	14a	drawing 22
b. photograph	14b	slide D.P.S. 3
c. relief[3]		drawing 20a
2. Funerary Texts		
a. photograph	15	OI photo 10329
b. hand copies	16–27	lines 1–120
(1) register A (top): lines 1–40	16–21	
(2) register B (middle): lines 41–80	22–24[4]	
(3) register C (bottom): lines 81–120	25–27	
B. West Wall		
1. Diagram	28a	drawing 23
a. partially destroyed inscription	28b	drawing 20b
2. Relief, upper section of wall		
a. photographs		
(1) upper third	29a–e	slides 49(south)–53(north)
(2) middle part	30	slides 54(south)–58(north)
b. composite drawing	31	drawings 15–19
c. details		
(1) *Ḥsw*, north end	32	slide 80
		drawing 15
(2) fowlers with net, north end	33	slide 88
		drawing 17[5]
(3) *Ḥsw*, fowling in the marshes, north to middle	34	slide 78
		drawing 16
(4) butchering and plowing, middle	35a–c	slides 56, 86, 87
	35d	drawing 18[6]
(5) *Ḥsw* and musicians, south end	36a	slide 59
	36b	drawing 19[7]
3. Funerary Texts		
a. photographs		
(1) north end	37	OI photo 10332
(a) register A (top): lines 121–168		
(b) register B (middle): lines 255–302		
(c) register C (bottom): lines 389–436		

---

on Egyptian Middle Kingdom Coffins and Related Documents (Berkeley: B.C. Scribe Publications, 1979), p. 57, where KH 1 KH is the designation of the tomb chamber of *Ḥsw*. Lesko, *ibid.*, pp. viii–ix, refers to the work of his predecessor T. G. Allen in regard to the sequences of funerary texts.

[3] The poor condition of the wall precluded the preparation of a facsimile drawing or an adequate slide; the drawing presented here is based on one in Edgar's original report, "Recent Discoveries at Kom el-Ḥisn," in G. Maspero, *Le Musée Égyptien: Recuil de Monuments et de Notices sur les Fouille d'Égypte III* (Cairo: l'Institut Français d'Archéologie Orientale, 1915), fig. 4. Cf. OI photograph 10329 in fig. 15.

[4] Lines 78–92 comprise a spell that begins in register B and continues in register C. There are a few cases where the end of a register does not correspond with the end of a spell; the hand copies, although following the orientation of the texts as they appear on the walls, are grouped according to particular spell.

[5] Cf. OI photograph 10332 and fig. 37.

[6] Cf. OI photograph 10331 and fig. 38

[7] Cf. OI photograph 10330 and fig. 39.

---

[8] The numbers listed T.G.A., beginning with line 432 and ending with line 522, refer to some of the numeration designated by T. G. Allen. We have followed the consistent pattern of numbering consecutively, north to south, throughout each register of the West wall.

[9] Lines 120–125 comprise a spell that begins in the last line of register C on the South wall and continues in register A on the West wall.

[10] Cf. OI photograph 10335 (fig. 94) and 10334 (fig. 100).

[11] Lines 559–583 comprise a spell that begins in register A and continues in register B.

	Figure	Reference

           (b) register B (middle): lines 568–615

           (c) register C (bottom): lines 647–694

     (2) middle[12]   100   OI photo 10334

           (a) register A (top): lines 553–567[13]

           (b) register B (middle): lines 598–646

           (c) register C (bottom): lines 677–724

     (3) south end   101   OI photo 10337

           (a) register A (top): lines 725–752

           (b) register B (middle): lines 753–780

           (c) register C (bottom): lines 781–808

   b. hand copies   102–126   lines 523–808

     (1) north end to middle[14]   102–118

           (a) register A (top): lines 523–567[15]   102–105

           (b) register B (middle): lines 568–646   106–112

           (c) register C (bottom): lines 647–724   113–118

     (2) south end   119–126

           (a) register A (top): lines 725–752   119–121

           (b) register B (middle): lines 753–780   122–123

           (c) register C (bottom): lines 781–808   124–126

D. Ceiling[16]

   1. Photograph   127a–e   slides 67–71

   2. Hand Copies   128–131   lines 809–815

     a. lines 809–810   128

     b. lines 811–812   129

     c. lines 813–814   130

     d. lines 815   131

---

[12] The photograph that illustrates this section also shows many lines from the north end.

[13] See note 11 above.

[14] The layout of inscriptions on this wall differs from that on the South and West walls in that the texts here do not continue across the wall from end to end in each consecutive horizontal register. The columns behind the figure of *Ḥsw* (see fig. 99), the table of offerings, and the recess interrupt the text. Register A ends below the figure of the tomb owner; then the text continues in Register B from the North end to just below the table of offerings. It then goes back to the North end in Register C and continues to the edge of the recess (see figs. 99–101).

[15] Lines 559–583 comprise a spell that begins in Register A and continues in Register B.

[16] The ceiling contains only seven columns of texts, but the hieroglyphs are larger and more finely carved and detailed than those used in the other funerary texts. Each line, while composed of passages from other funerary texts, appears to be complete in itself; it does not continue to the next column. The hand copies here are broken up into smaller columns to accommodate the format used throughout the book. Some of the corrections in the damaged areas are based on the readings supplied by Edgar, "Recent Discoveries," p. 60

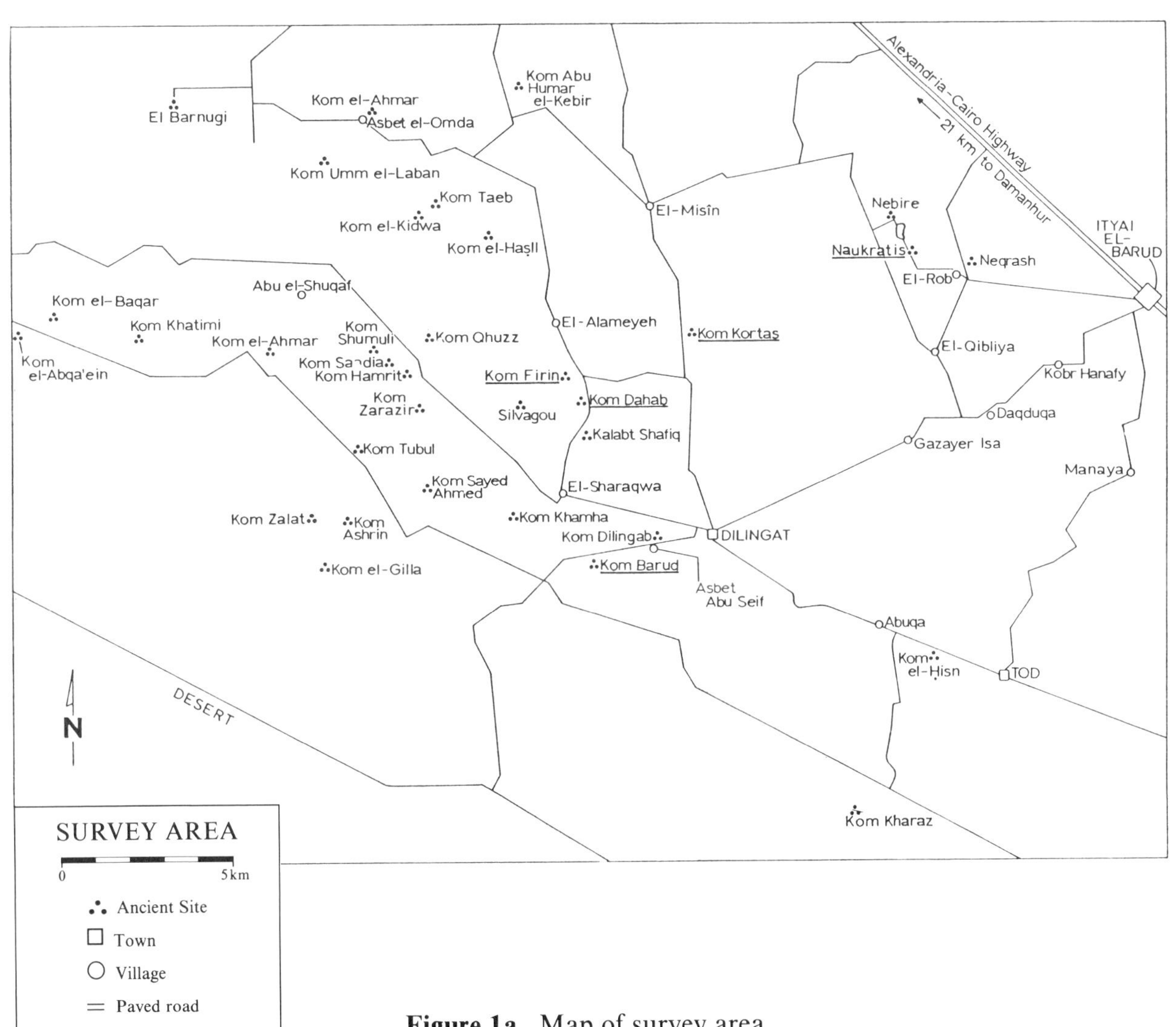

Figure 1a. Map of survey area.

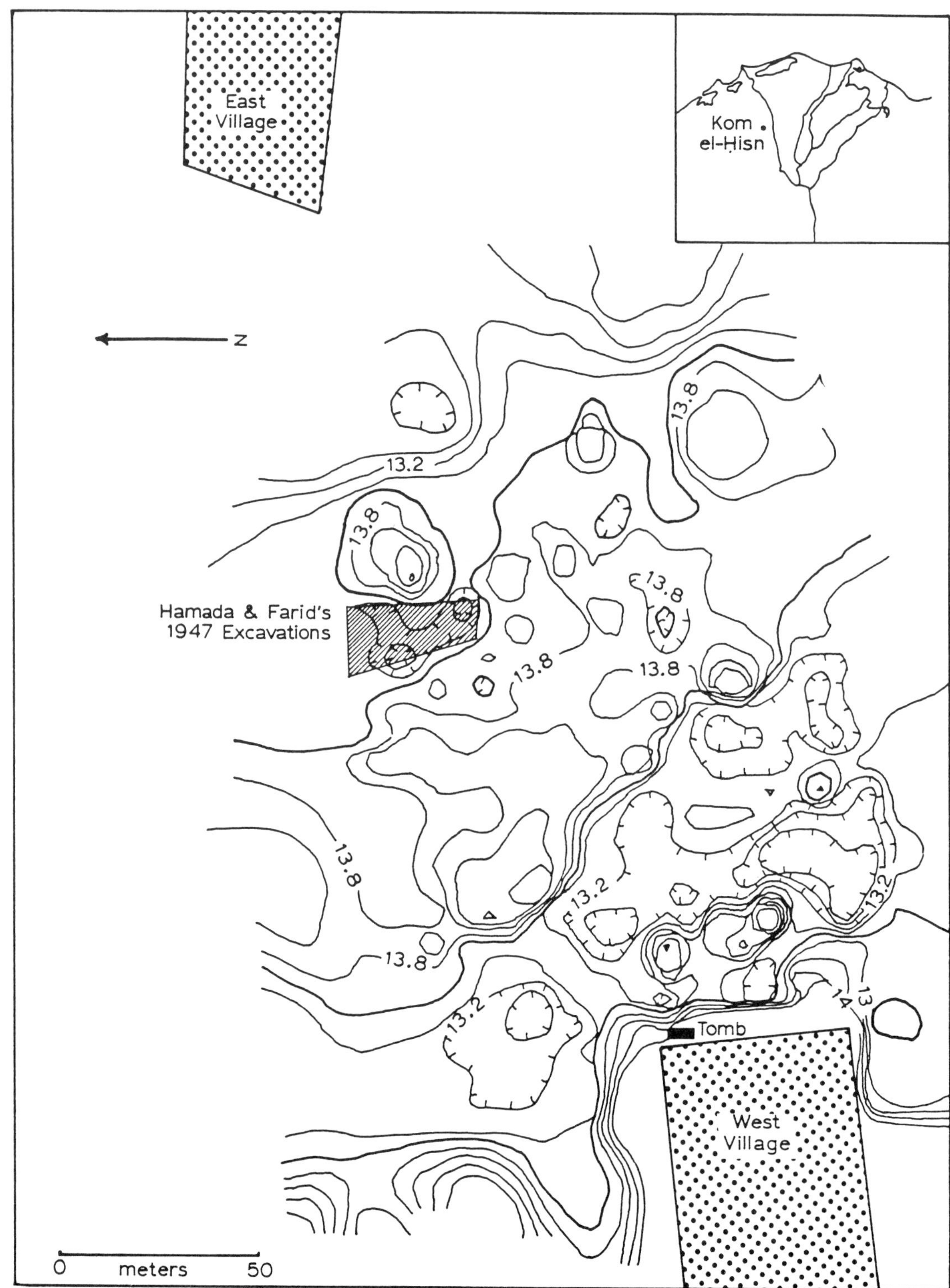

Figure 1b. Topographical map of survey area.

Figure 2. View of the area of Kom el-Ḥisn, looking south.

Figure 3. Plan of the tomb at Kom el-Ḥisn.

Figure 4. View of the tomb, inside protective housing, looking north.

Figure 5. Exterior view of the tomb chamber, looking north.

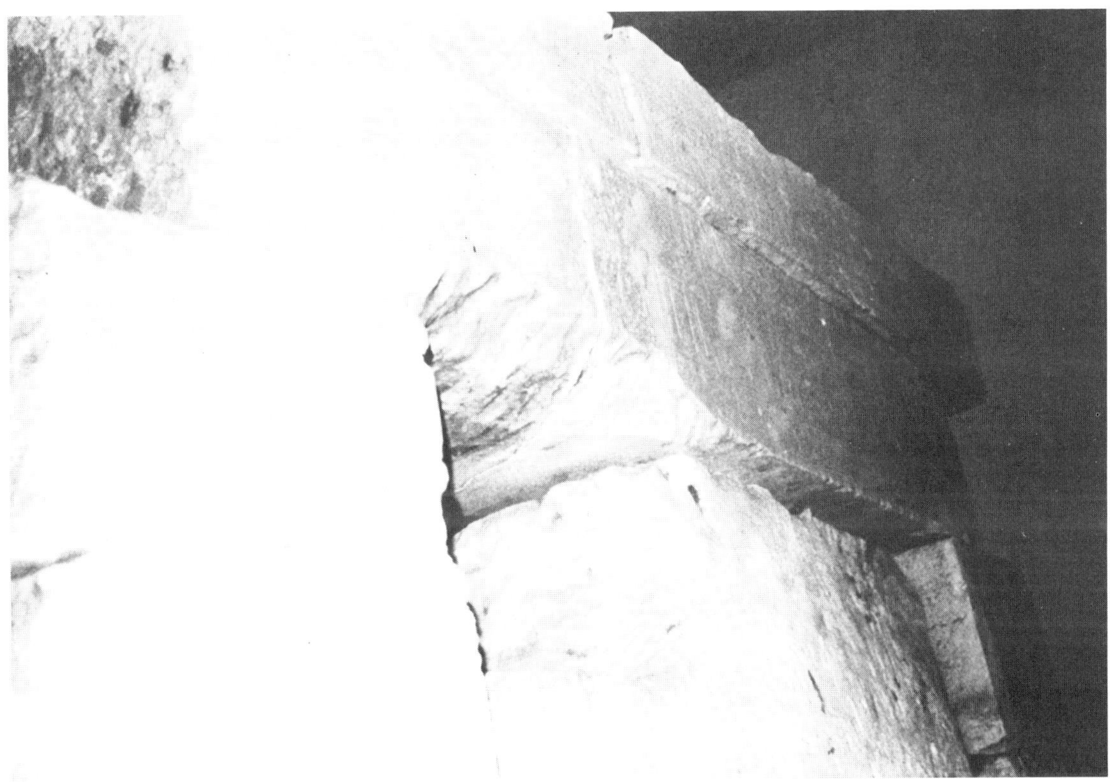

Figure 6a. Overall view of the northern façade.

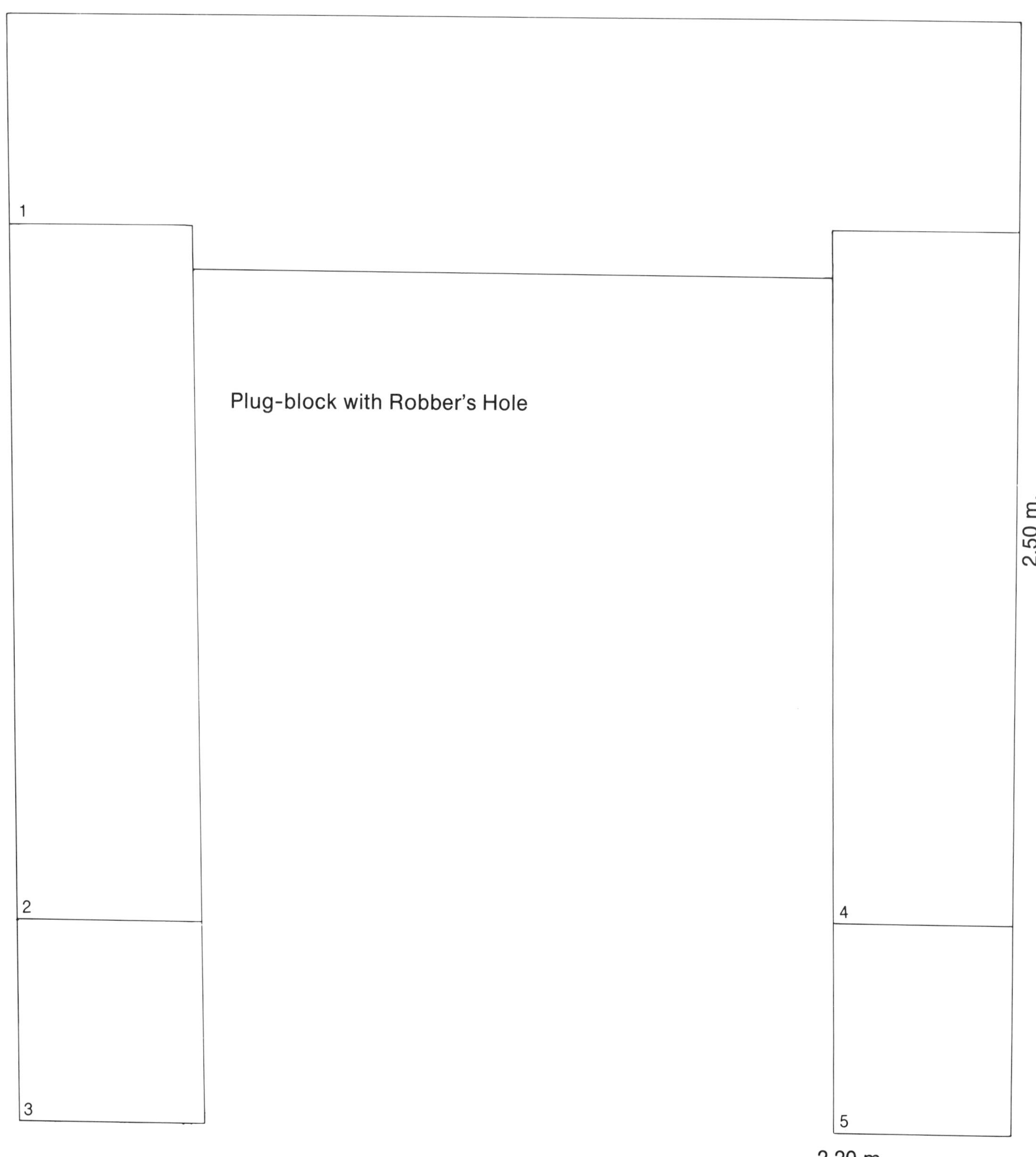

Figure 6b. Schematic drawing of façade (north wall, exterior).

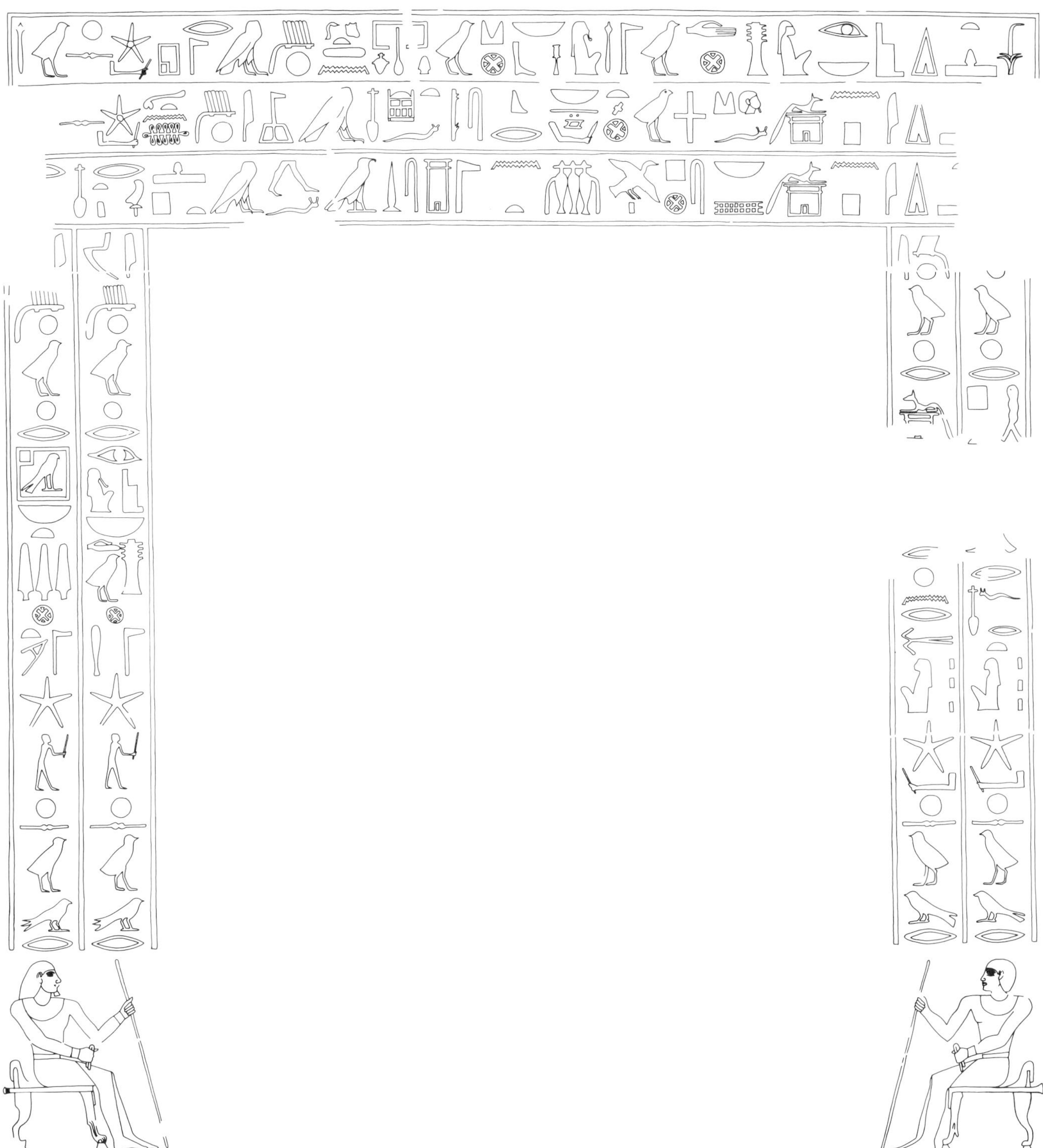

Figure 7. Composite drawing of the northern façade.

Figure 8a–d. Photographs of the lintel, northern façade.

Figure 8e–g. Photographs of the lintel, northern façade.

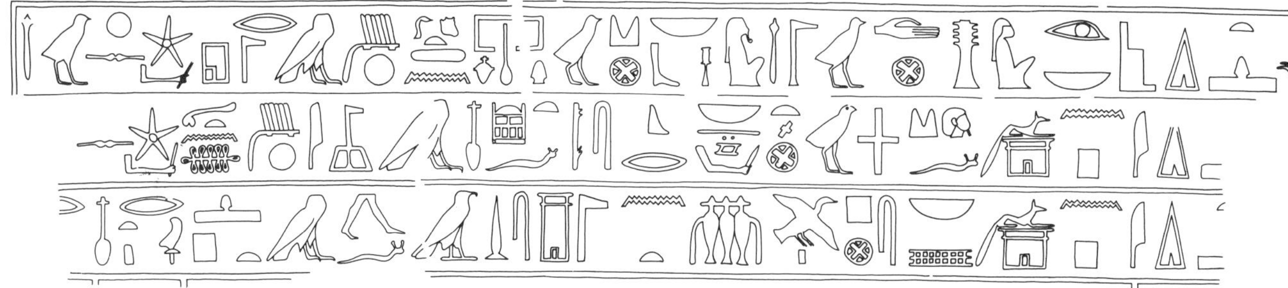

Figure 9. Drawing of the lintel, northern façade.

a.

b.

Figure 10a–b. Photographs of the left jamb (east), northern façade.

c.

d.

e.

Figure 10c–e. Photographs of the left jamb (east), northern façade.

f.

g.

Figure 10f–g. Photographs of the left jamb (east), northern façade.

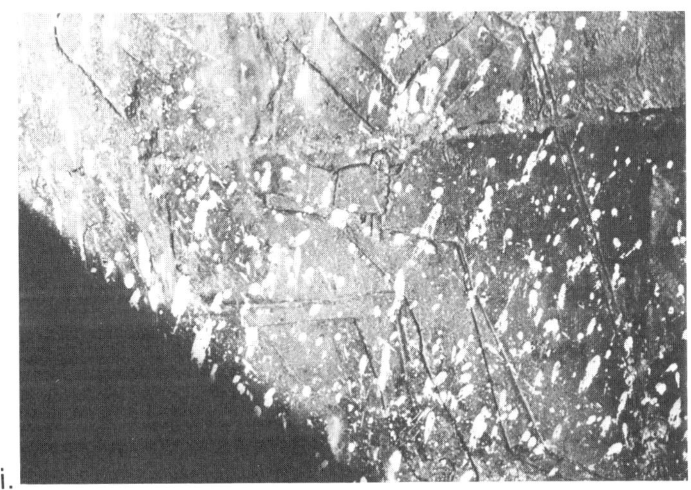

Figure 10h–i. Photograph of the left jamb (east), northern façade.

Figure 11a. Drawing of the left jamb (east), northern façade (lower part).

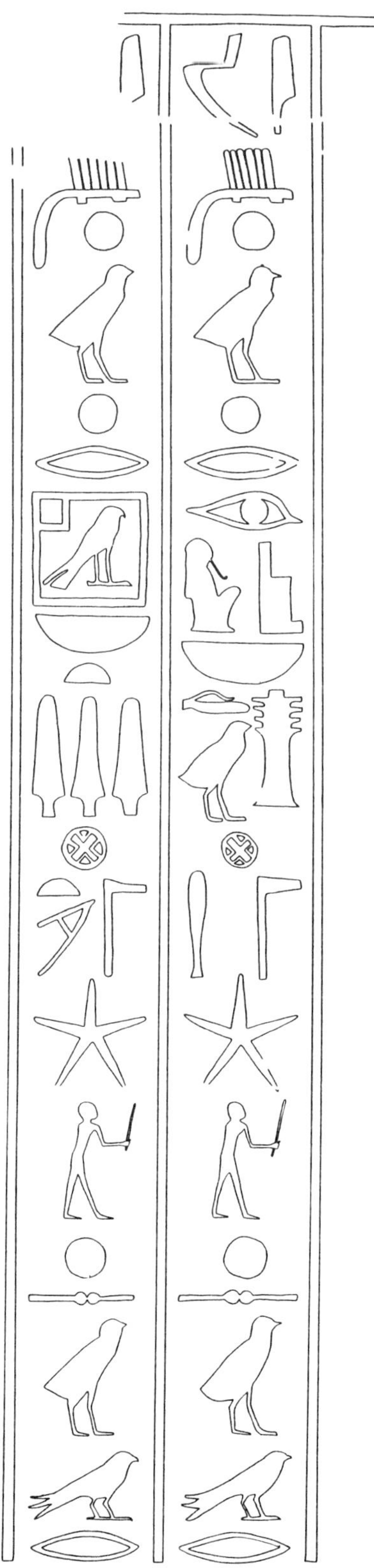

Figure 11b. Drawing of the left jamb (east), northern façade (upper part).

Figure 12a–c. Photographs of the right jamb (west), northern façade.

Figure 12d–f. Photographs of the right jamb (west), northern façade.

Figure 12g–h. Photographs of the right jamb (west), northern façade.

Figure 13a. Drawing of the right jamb (west), northern façade (lower portion).

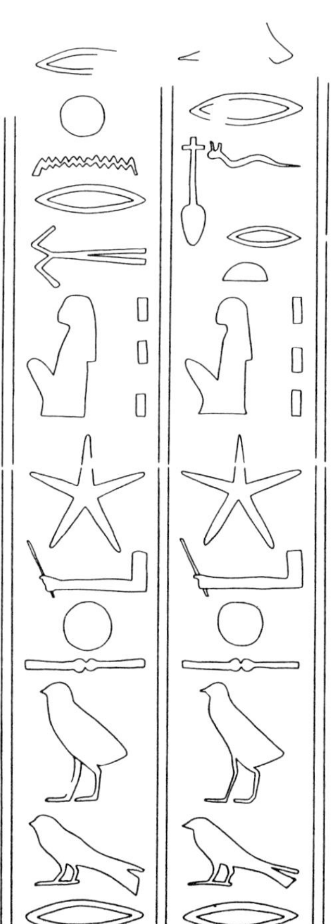

Figure 13b. Drawing of the right jamb (west), northern façade (upper portion).

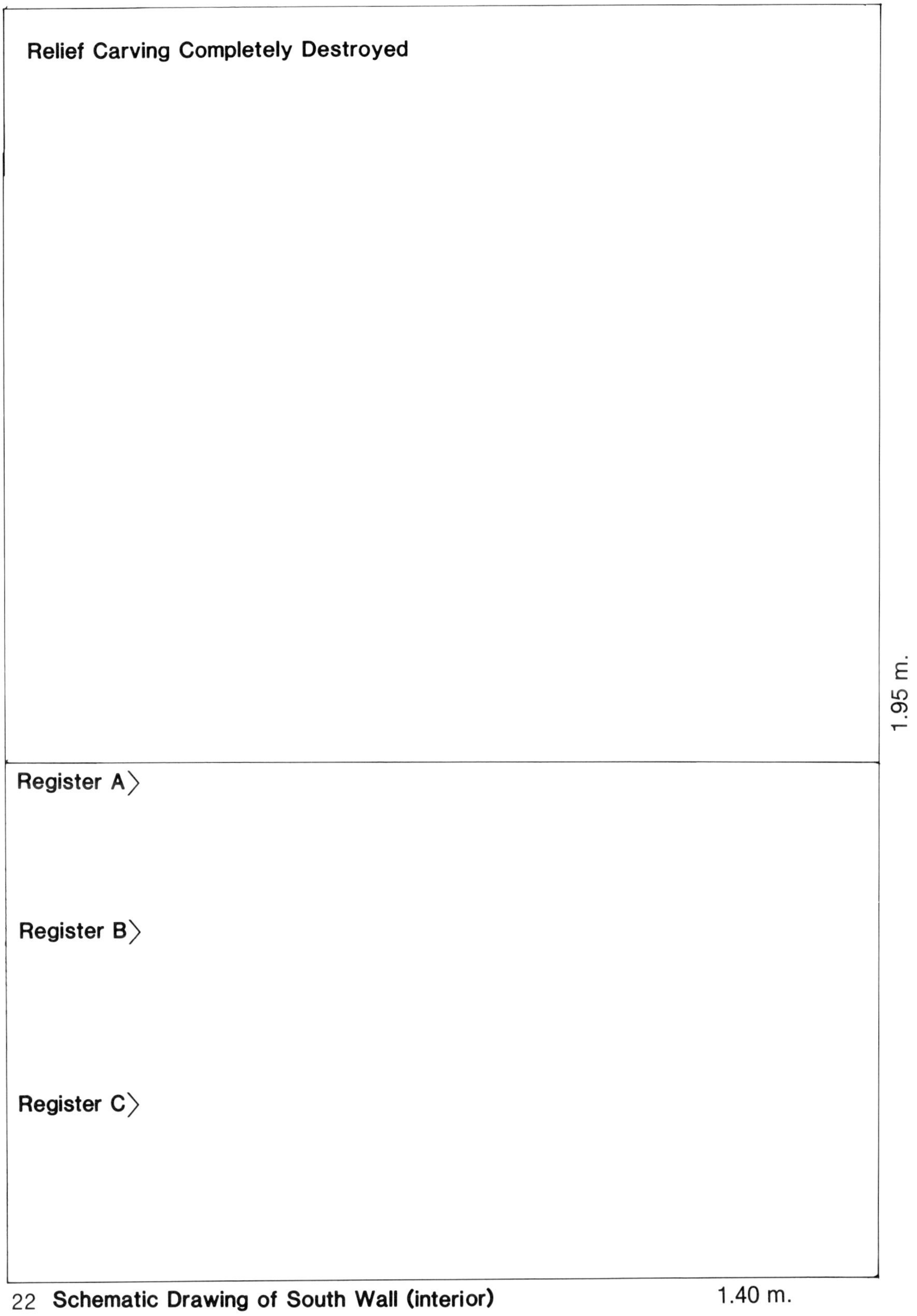

Relief Carving Completely Destroyed

1.95 m.

Register A⟩

Register B⟩

Register C⟩

22 **Schematic Drawing of South Wall (interior)**   1.40 m.

Figure 14a. Diagram of the south wall of the tomb chamber.

Figure 14b. Photograph of south wall of tomb chamber.

Figure 14c. Drawing of carved frieze now destroyed on upper part of south wall.

Figure 15. Photograph of the relief of funerary texts on the south wall. Courtesy of the Oriental Institute.

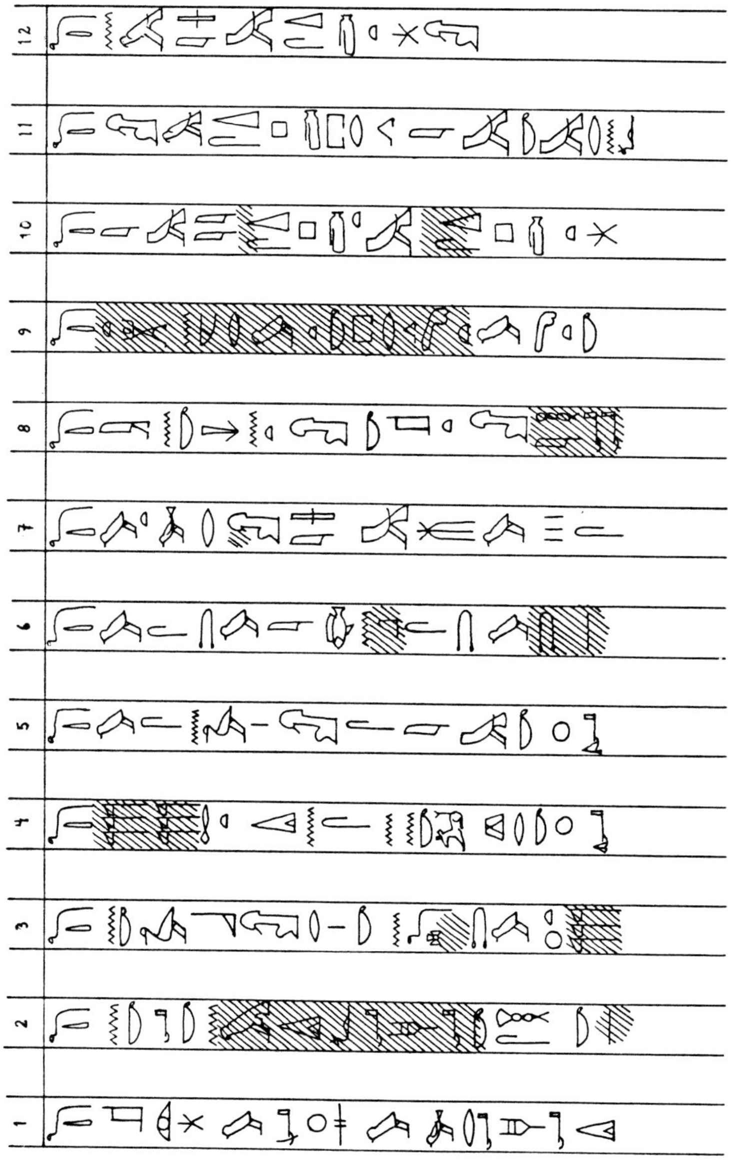

The Tomb Chamber of Ḥsw The Elder

Figure 16. Hand copy, Register A (top), lines 1–12.

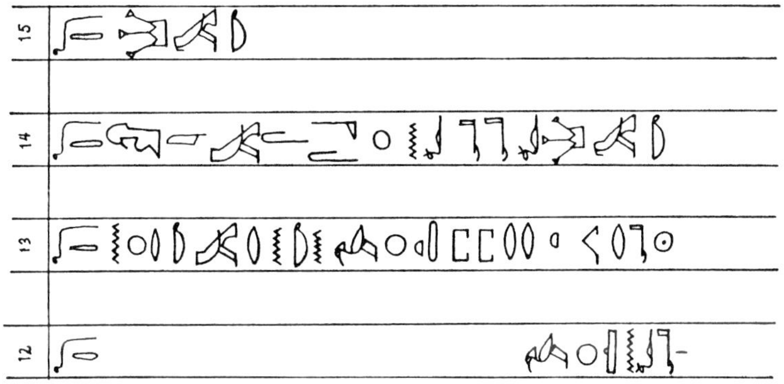

Figure 17. Hand copy, Register A (top), lines 12–15.

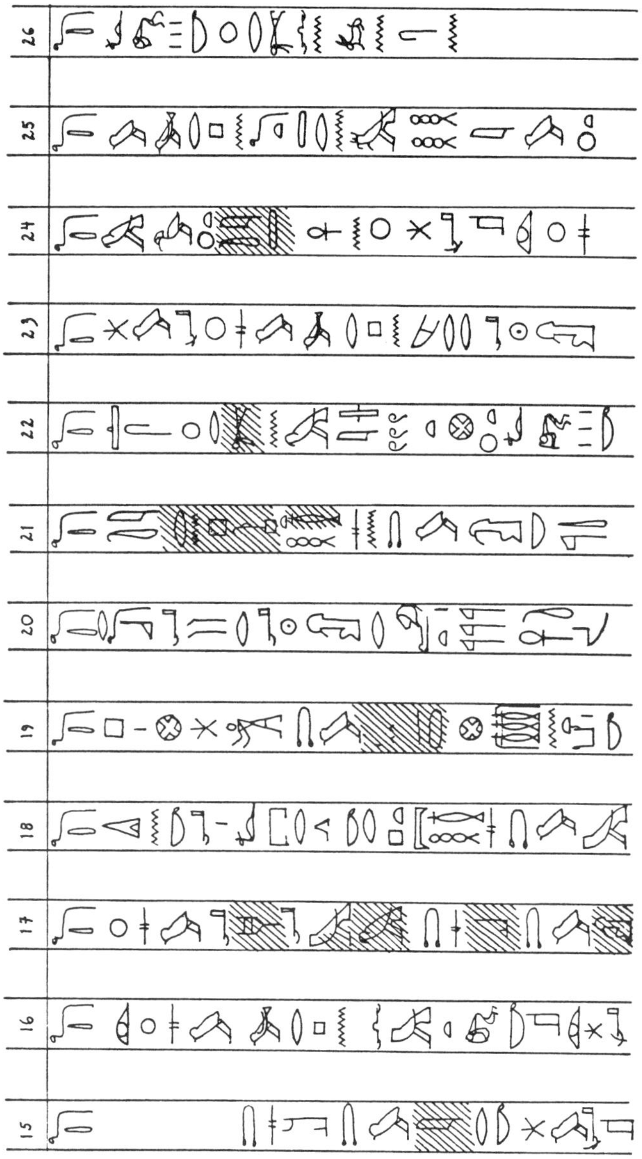

Figure 18. Hand copy, Register A (top), lines 15–26.

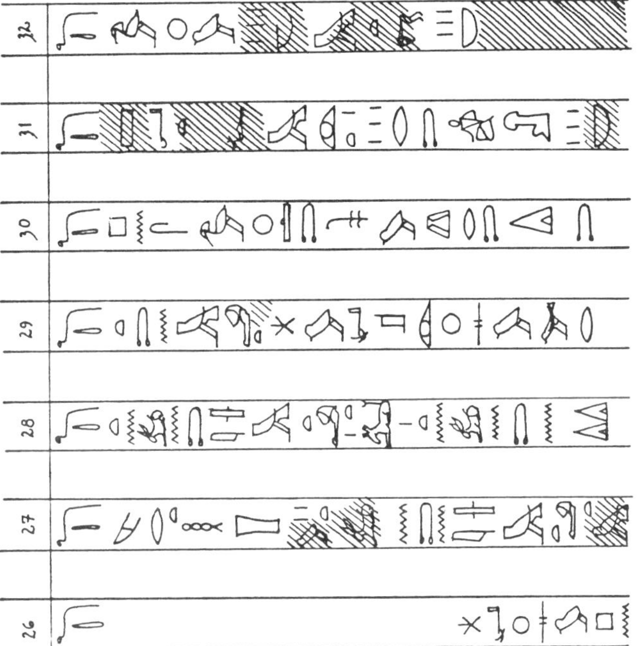

Figure 19. Hand copy, Register A (top), lines 26–32.

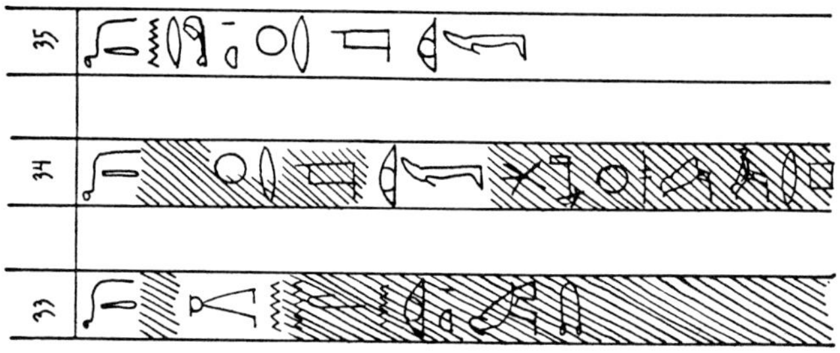

Figure 20. Hand copy, Register A (top), lines 33–35.

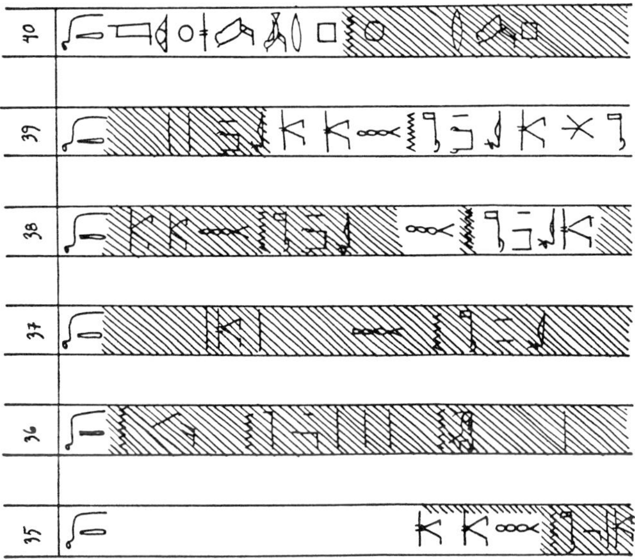

Figure 21. Hand copy, Register A (top), lines 35–40.

The Tomb Chamber of Ḥsw The Elder

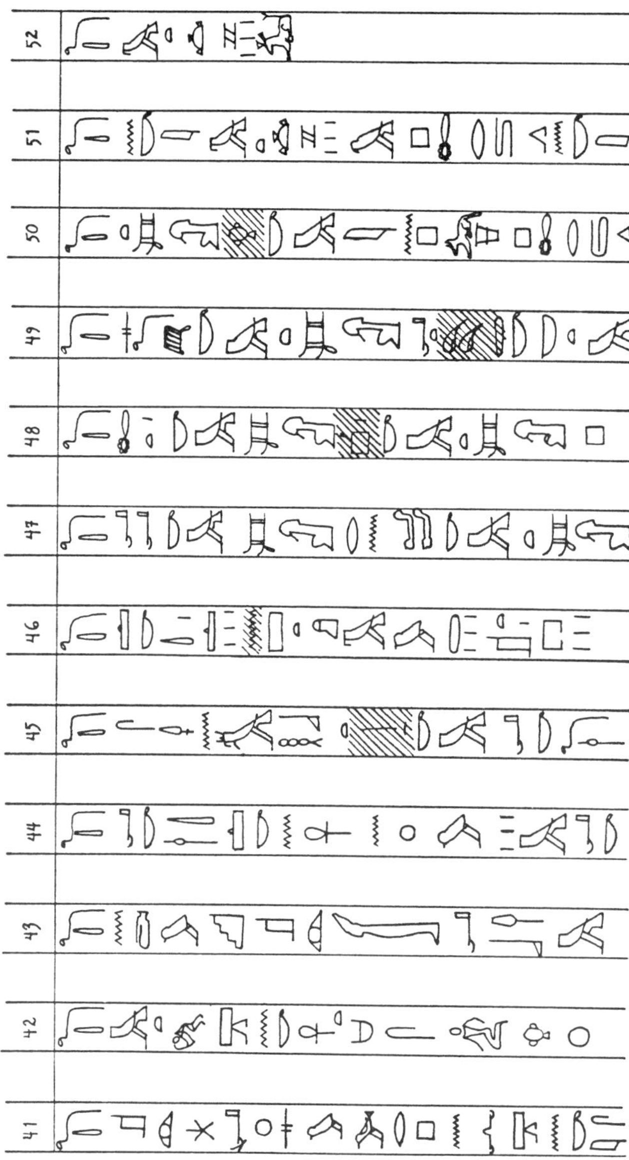

Figure 22. Hand copy, Register B (middle), lines 41–52.

Figure 23. Hand copy, Register B (middle), lines 52–78 (continued on figure 24).

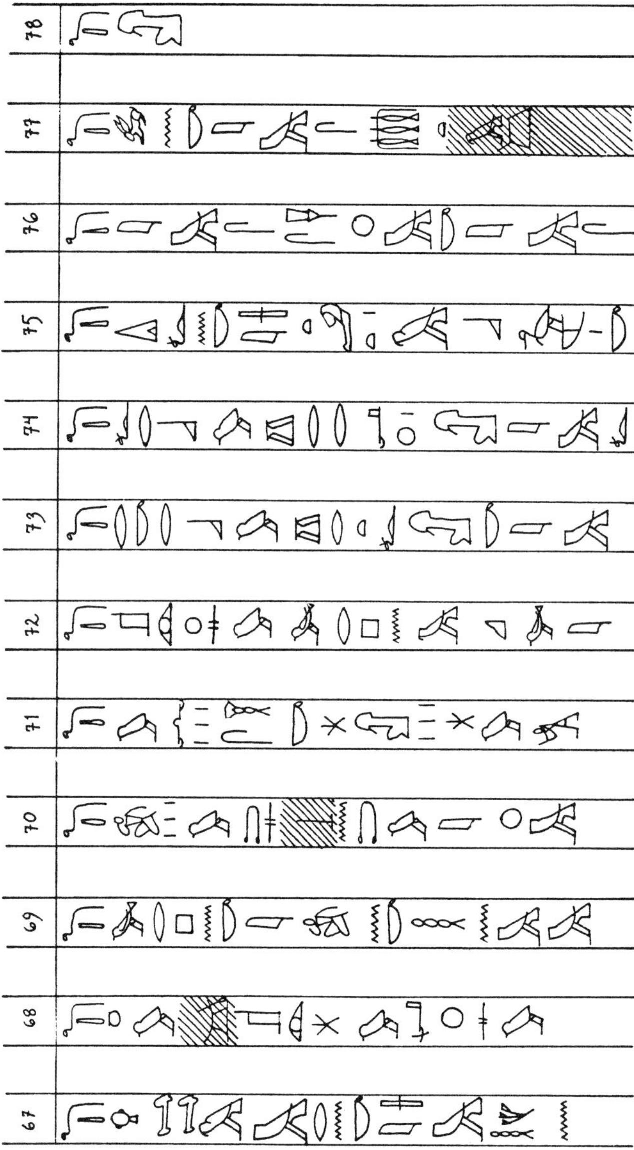

Figure 24. Hand copy, Register B (middle), lines 52–78 (continued from figure 23).

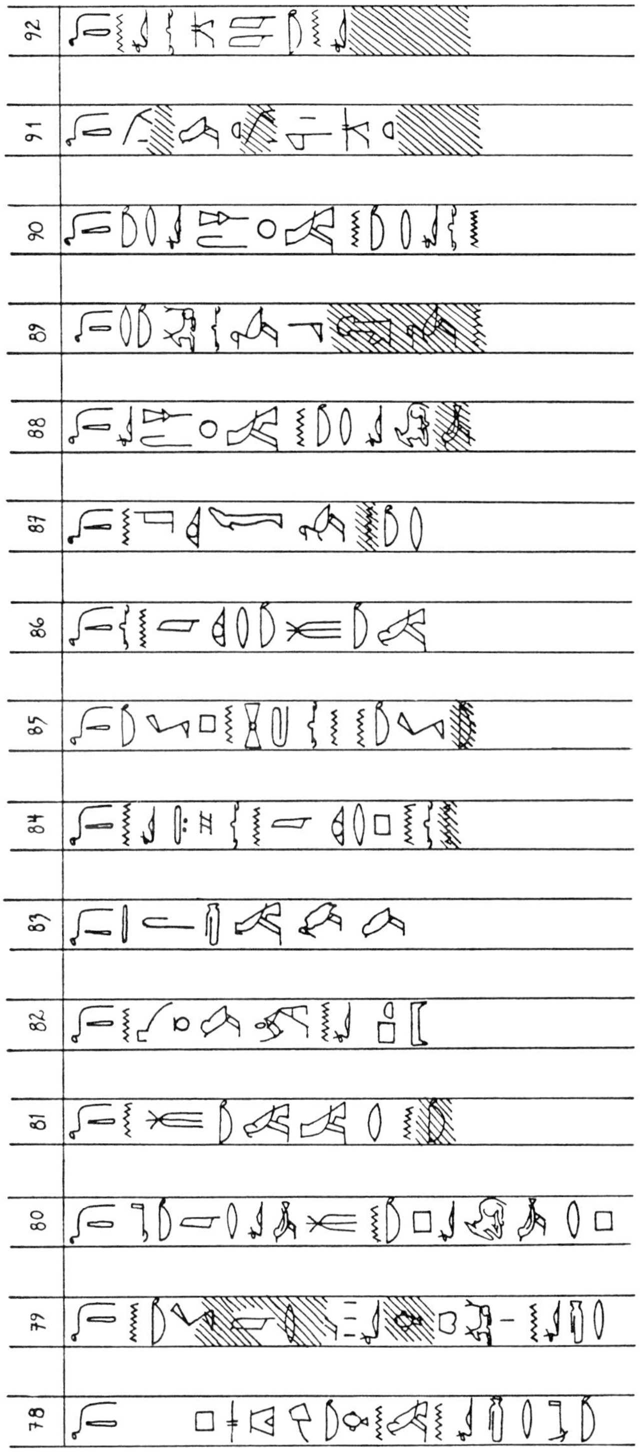

Figure 25. Hand copy, Registers B–C (middle-bottom), lines 78–92 (line 81 begins bottom register).

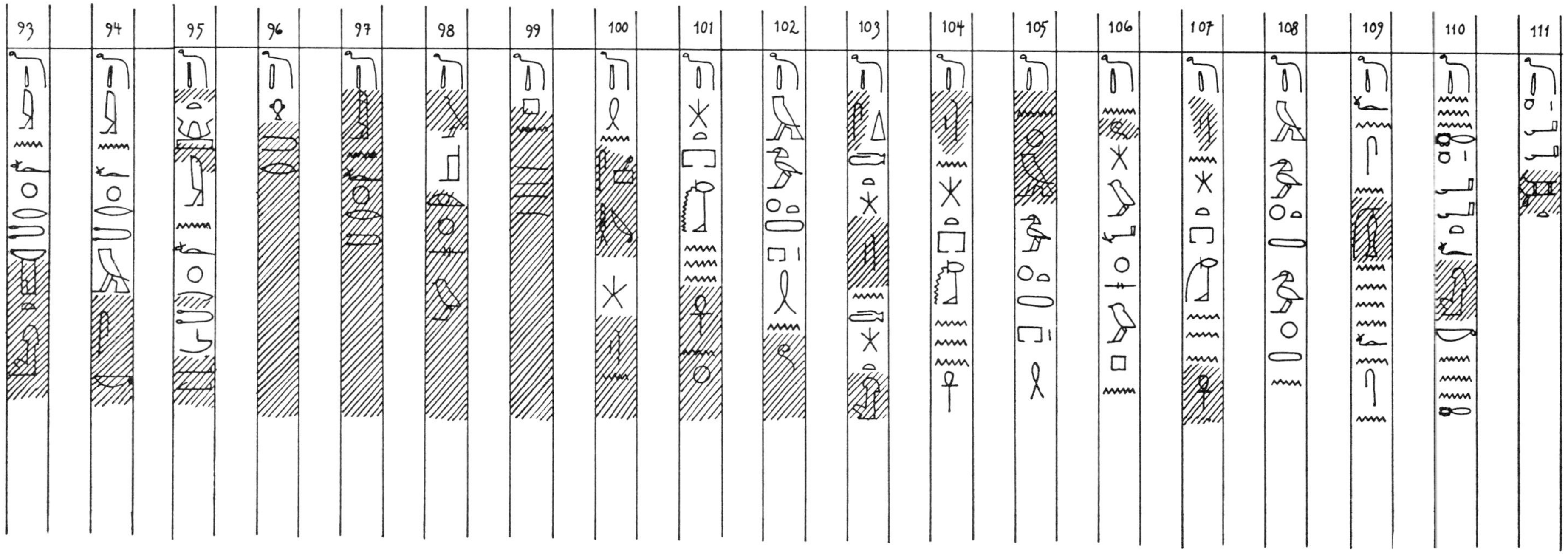

Figure 26. Hand copy, Register C (bottom), lines 93–111.

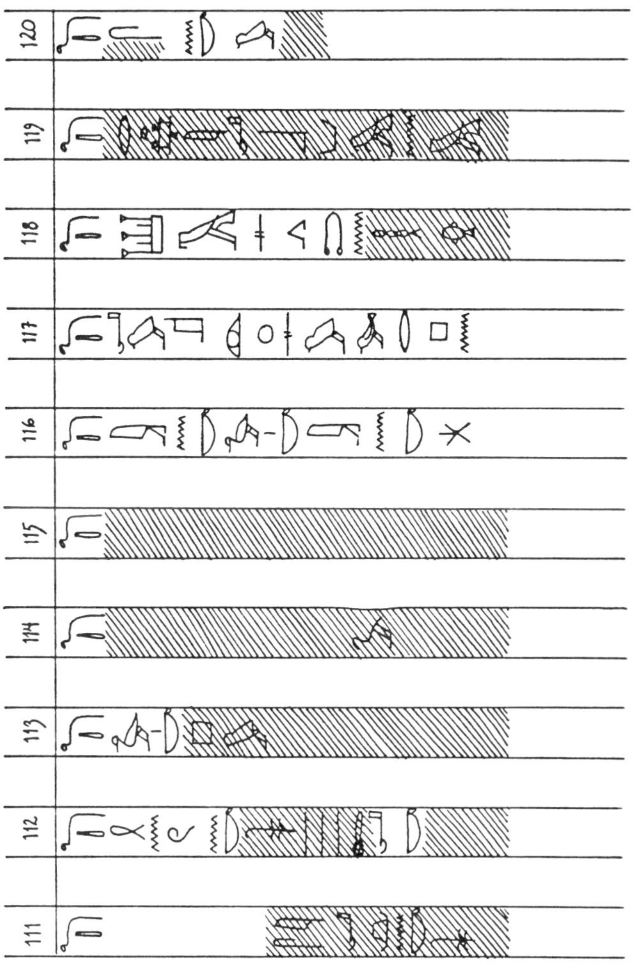

Figure 27. Hand copy, Register C (bottom), lines 111–120.

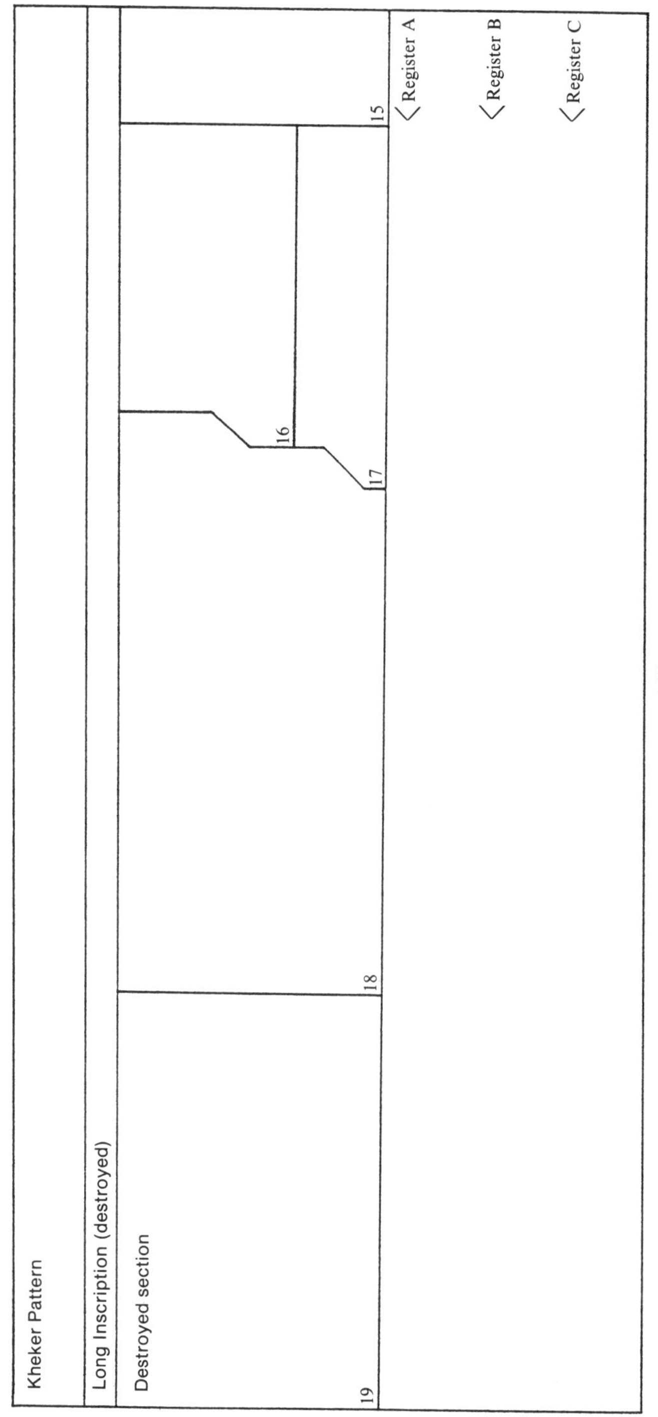

Figure 28a. Diagram of the west wall of the tomb chamber. (Interior numbers refer to drawings, cf. figure 31.)

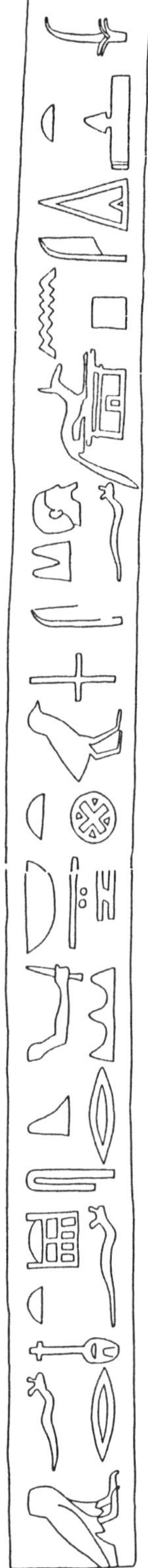

Figure 28b. Remains of partially destroyed inscription.

a.

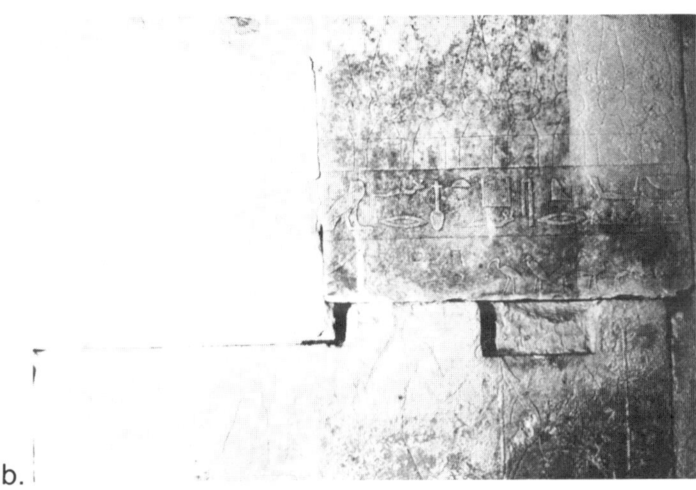

b.

c.

Figure 29a–c. Photographs of the upper section of the west wall (top).

Figure 29d–e. Photographs of the upper section of the west wall (top).

a.

b.

c.

Figure 30a–c. Photographs of the upper section of the west wall (middle).

Figure 30d–e. Photographs of the upper section of the west wall (middle).

Figure 31. Composite drawing of the relief, upper section of the west wall.

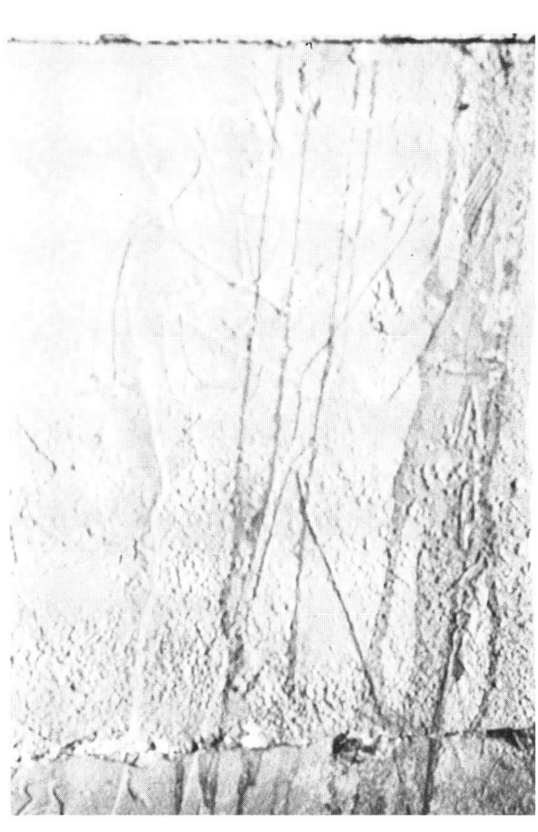

Figure 32. Drawing and photograph, *Ḥsw*, (north end of the relief on the west wall).

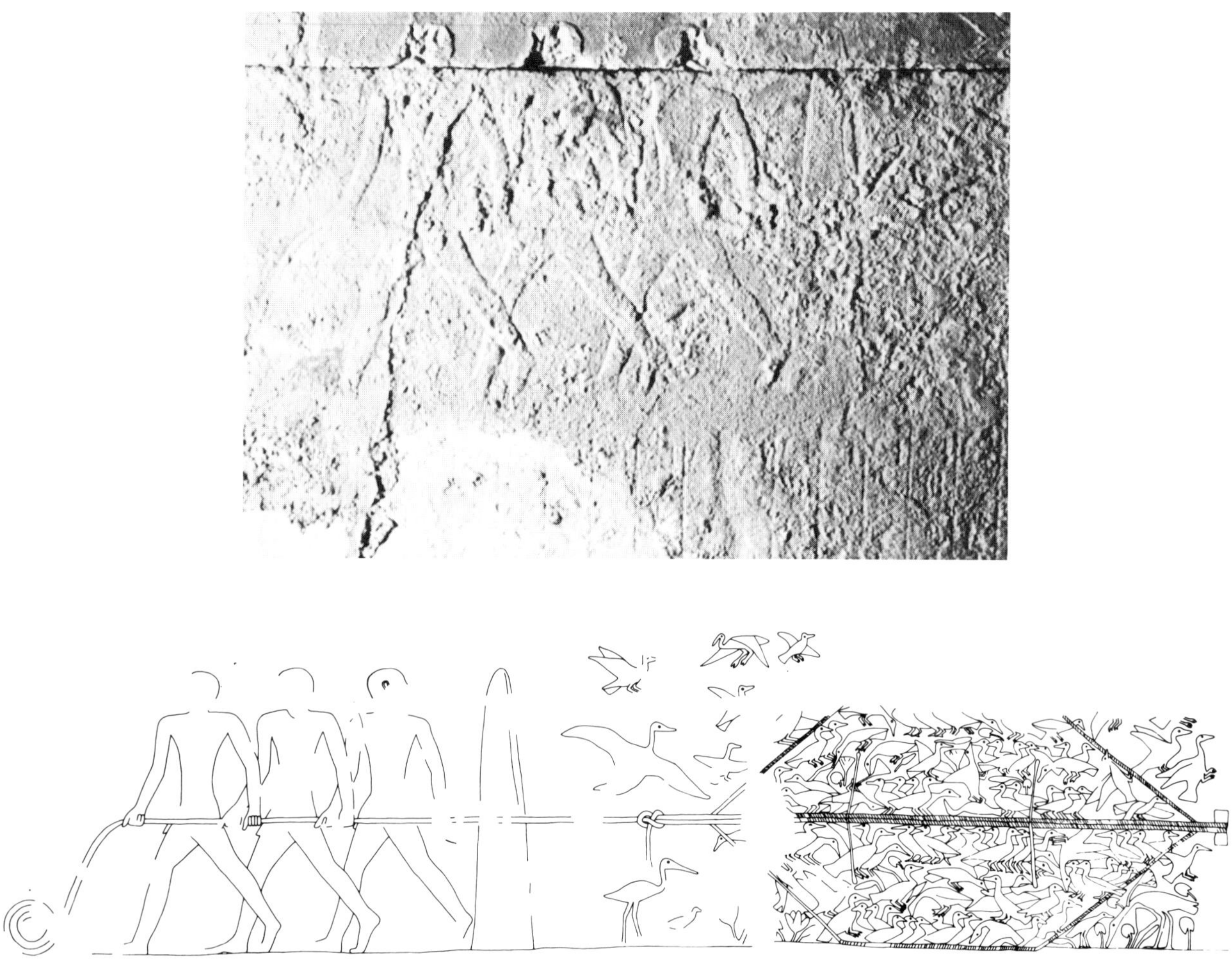

Figure 33. Photograph and drawing, fowlers with net (north end of the relief on the west wall).

Figure 34. Photograph and drawing, *Ḥsw*, fowling in the marshes (north to middle part of the relief on the west wall).

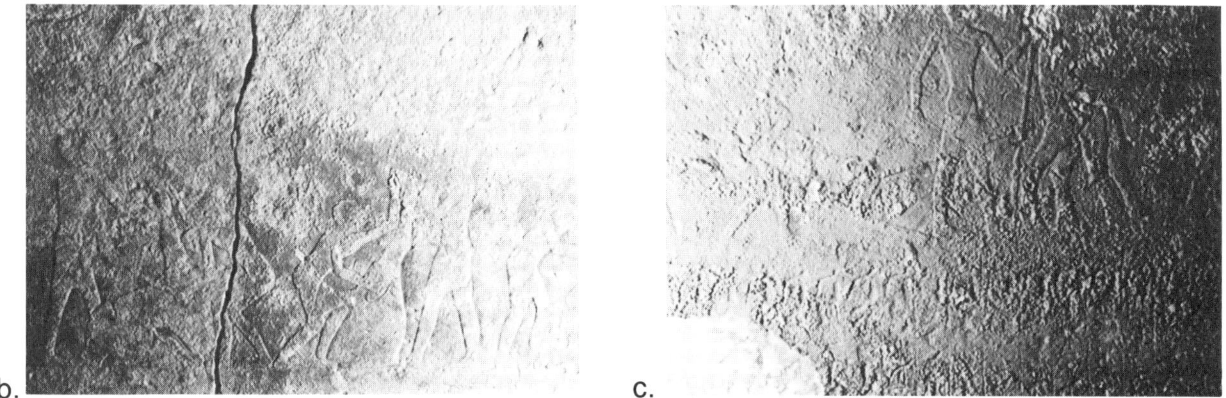

Figure 35a–c. Photographs of butchering and plowing, middle part of the relief on the west wall.

Figure 35d. Drawing of butchering and plowing, middle part of the relief on the west wall.

Figure 36a. Photograph, south part of the relief on the west wall.

Figure 36b. Drawing, far south, west wall.

Figure 37. Photograph of the north end of the funerary text on the west wall, showing Register A (top, lines 121–168), Register B (middle, lines 255–302), and Register C (bottom, lines 389–436). Courtesy of the Oriental Institute.

Figure 38. Photograph of the middle section of the funerary text on the west wall, showing Register A (top, lines 164–214), Register B (middle, lines 298–347), and Register C (bottom, lines 431–482). Courtesy of the Oriental Institute.

Figure 39. Photograph of the south end of the funerary text on the west wall, showing Register A (lines 210–254), Register B (middle, lines 344–388), and Register C (bottom, lines 477–522). Courtesy of the Oriental Institute.

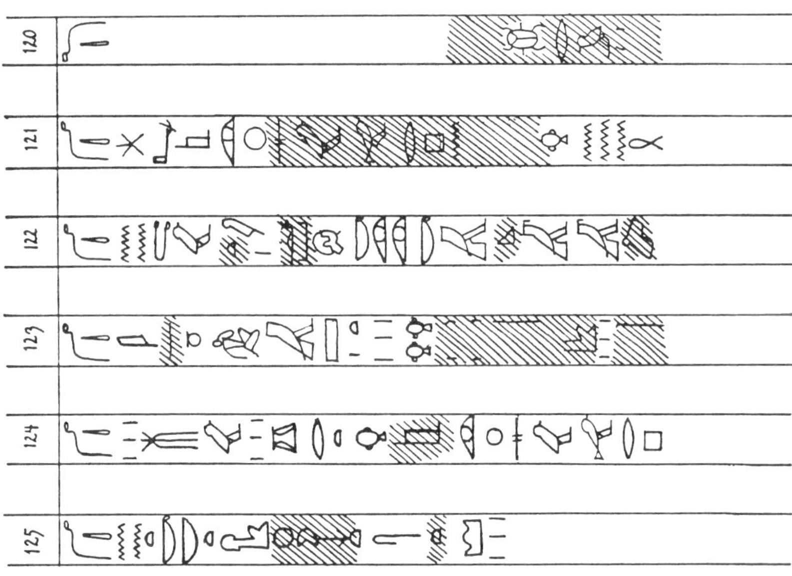

Figure 40. Hand copy, west wall, Register A, lines 120–125.

The Tomb Chamber of Ḥsw The Elder

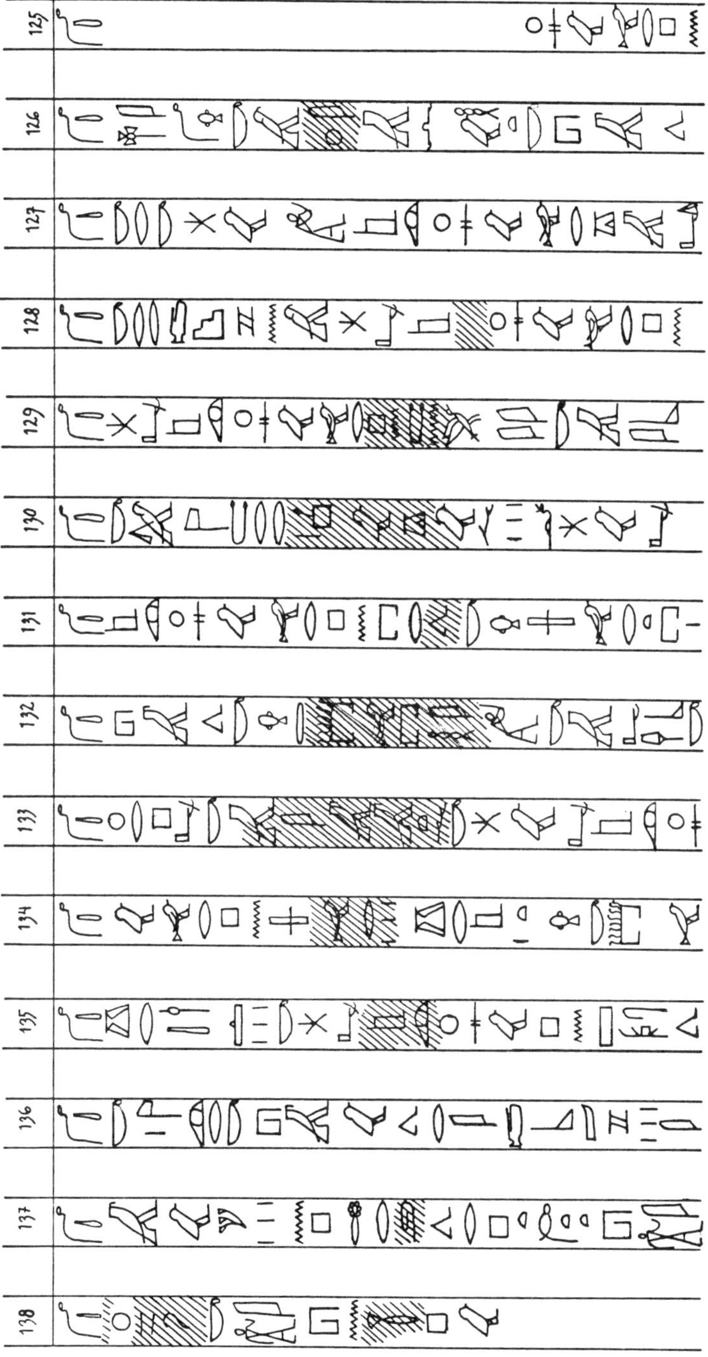

Figure 41. Hand copy, west wall, Register A, lines 125–138.

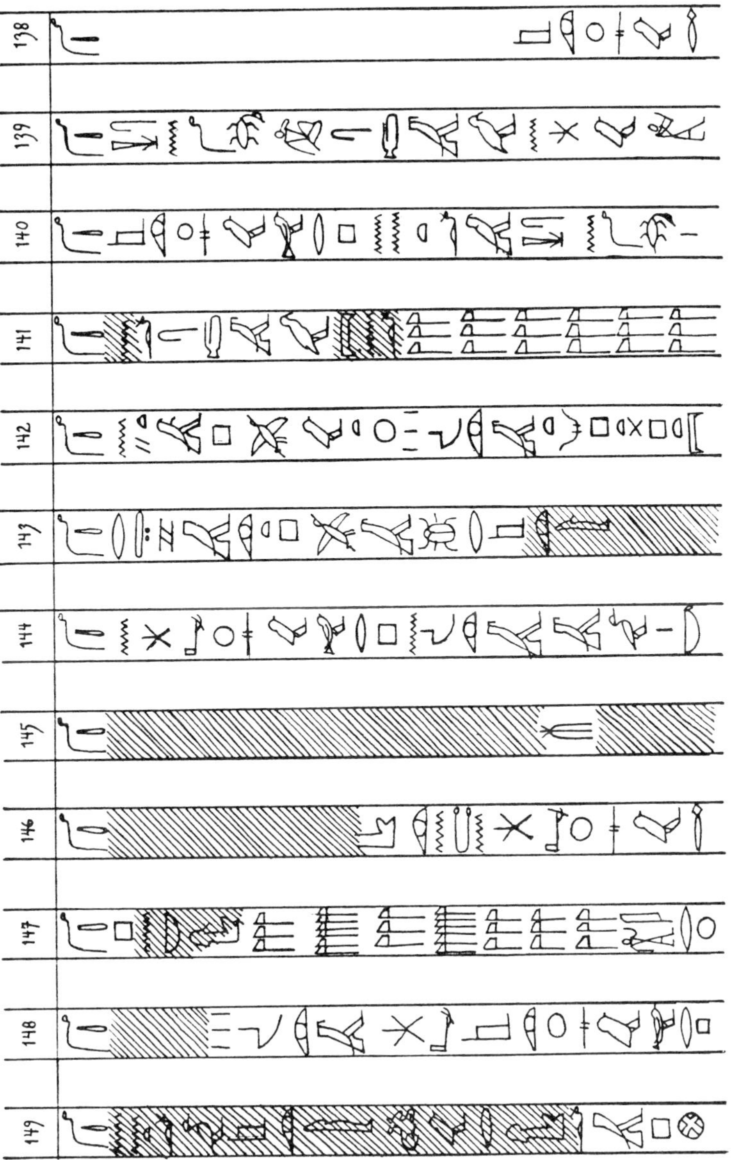

Figure 42. Hand copy, west wall, Register A, lines 138–158 (continued on figure 43).

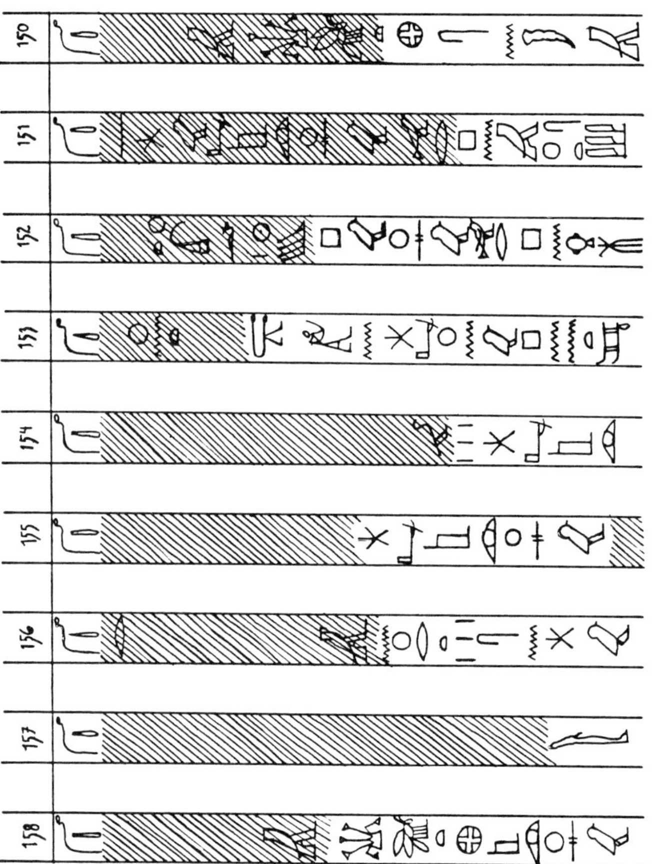

Figure 43. Hand copy, west wall, Register A, lines 138–158 (continued from figure 42).

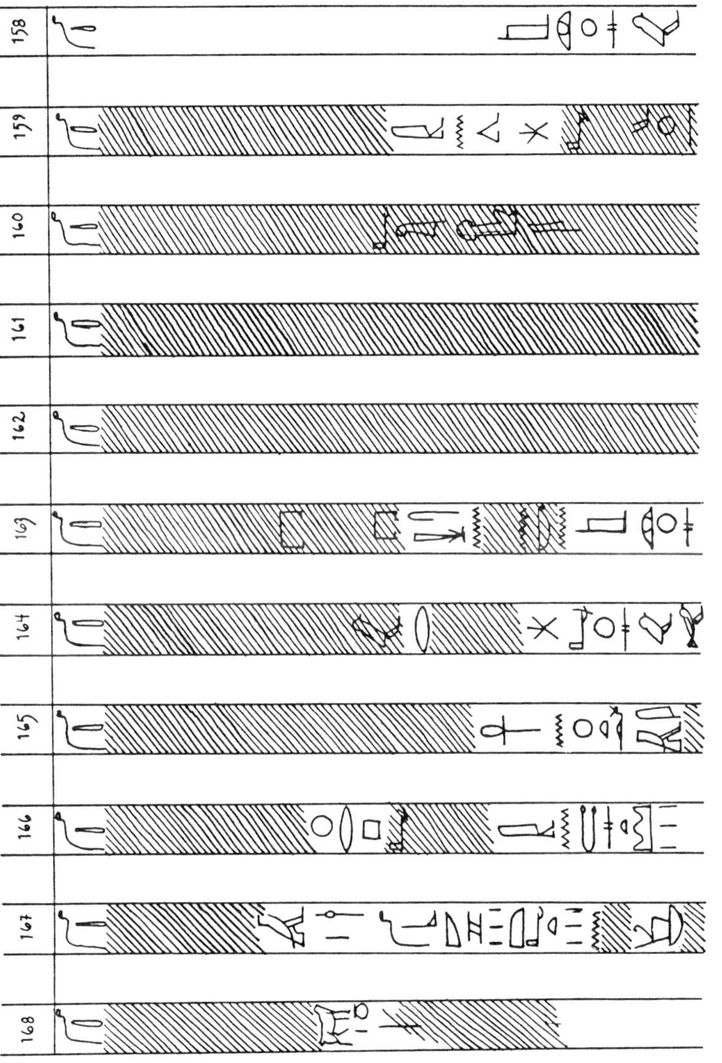

Figure 44. Hand copy, west wall, Register A, lines 158–168.

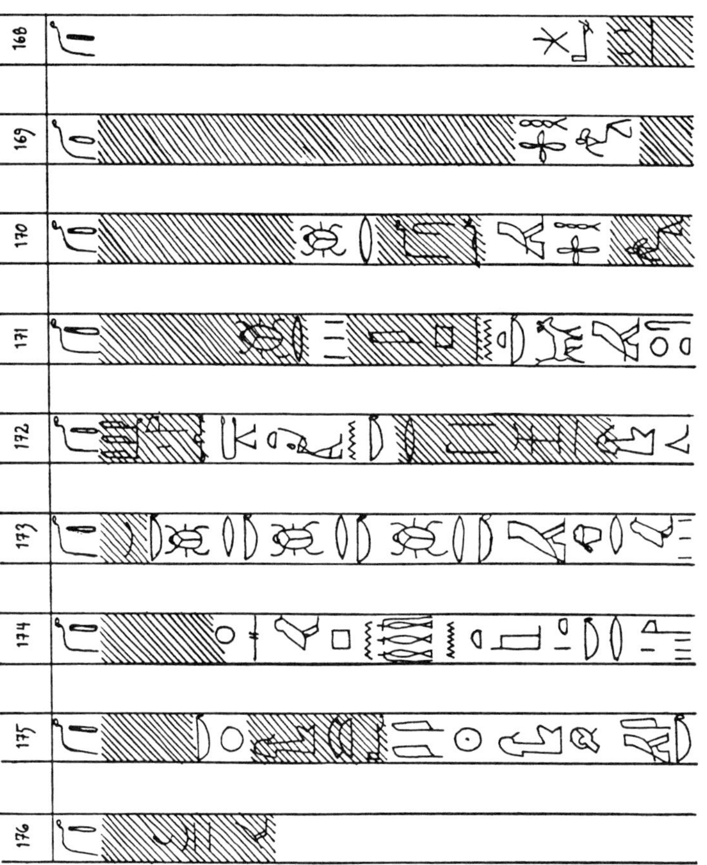

Figure 45. Hand copy, west wall, Register A, lines 168–176.

Figure 46. Hand copy, west wall, Register A, lines 176–183.

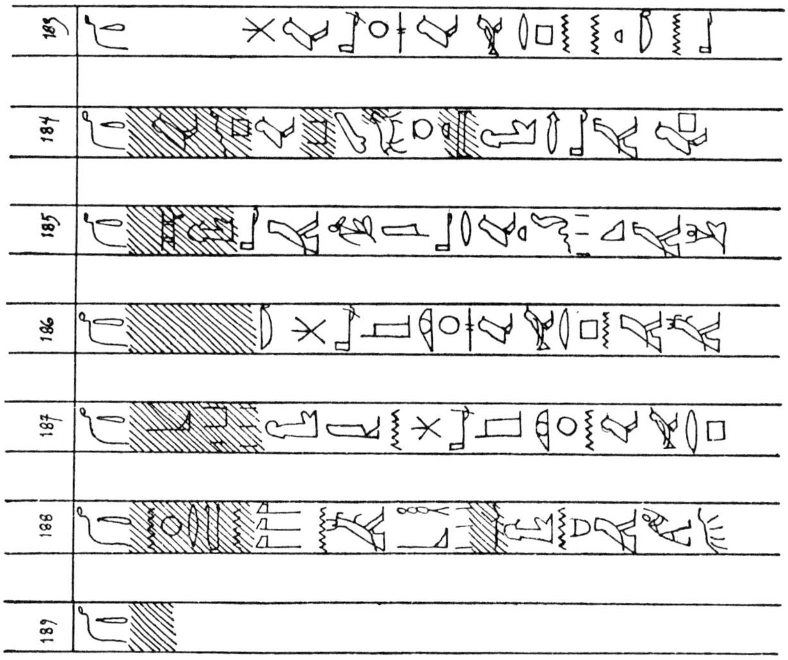

The Tomb Chamber of Ḥsw The Elder

Figure 47. Hand copy, west wall, Register A, lines 183–189.

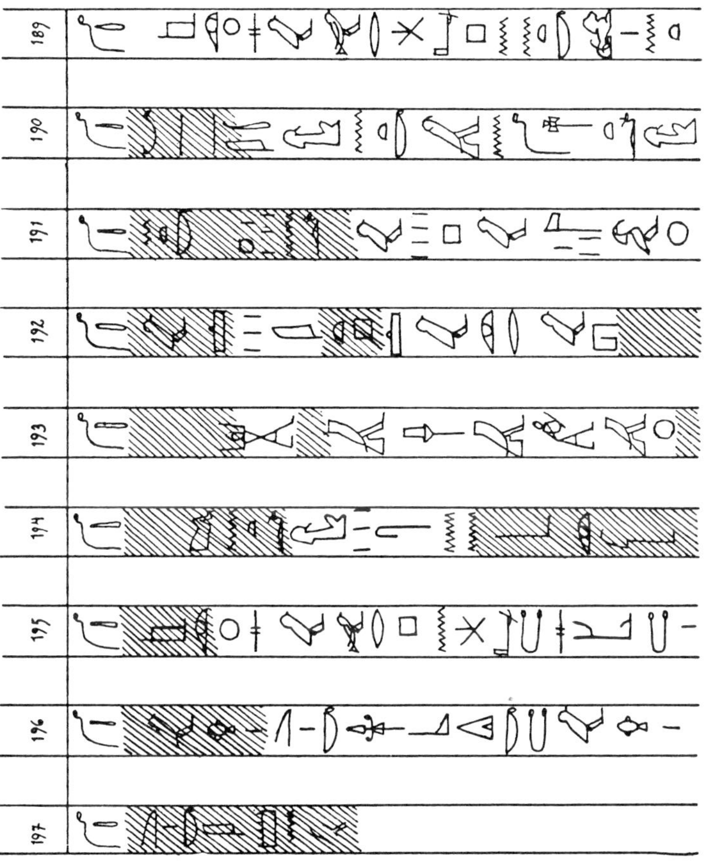

Figure 48. Hand copy, west wall, Register A, lines 189–197.

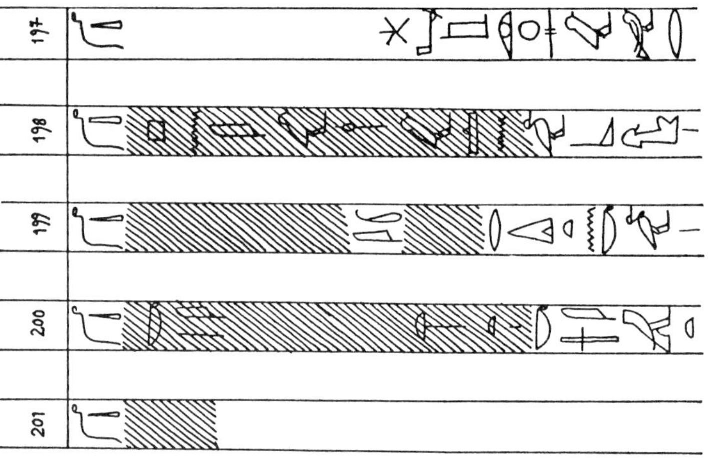

Figure 49. Hand copy, west wall, Register A, lines 197–201.

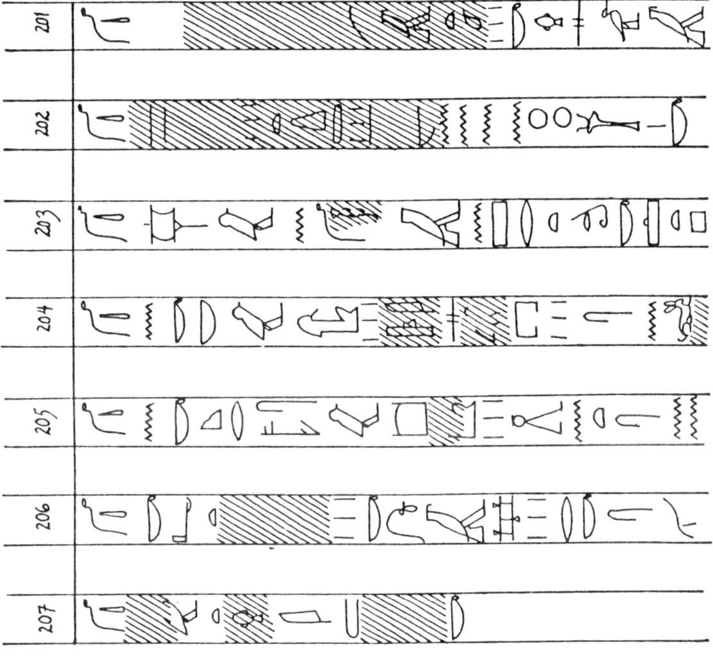

Figure 50. Hand copy, west wall, Register A, lines 201–207.

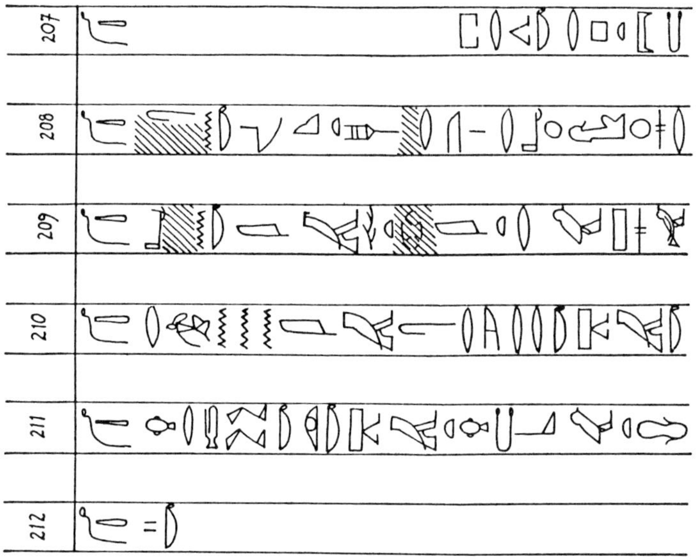

Figure 51. Hand copy, west wall, Register A, lines 207–212.

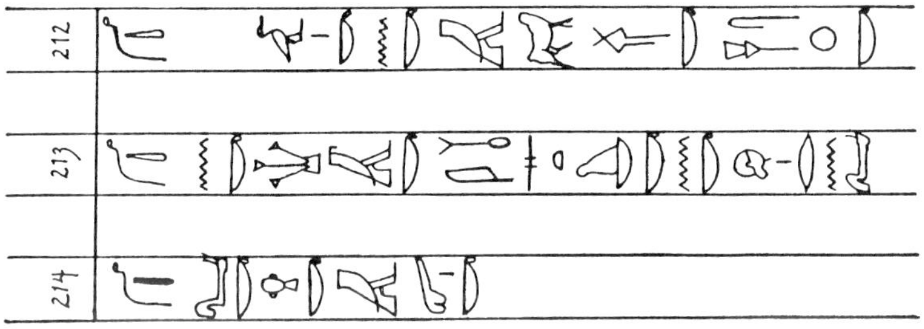

Figure 52. Hand copy, west wall, Register A, lines 212–214.

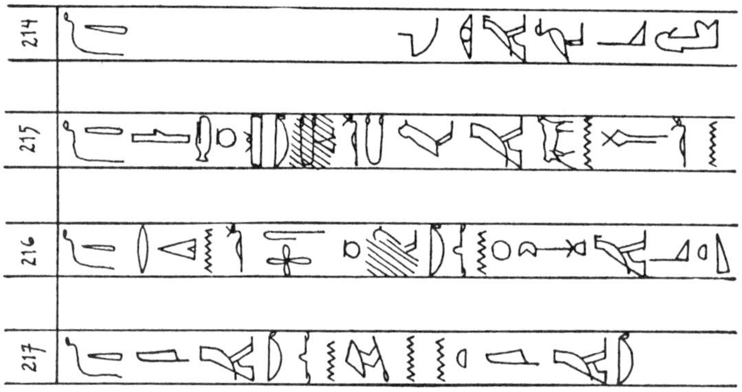

Figure 53. Hand copy, west wall, Register A, lines 214–217.

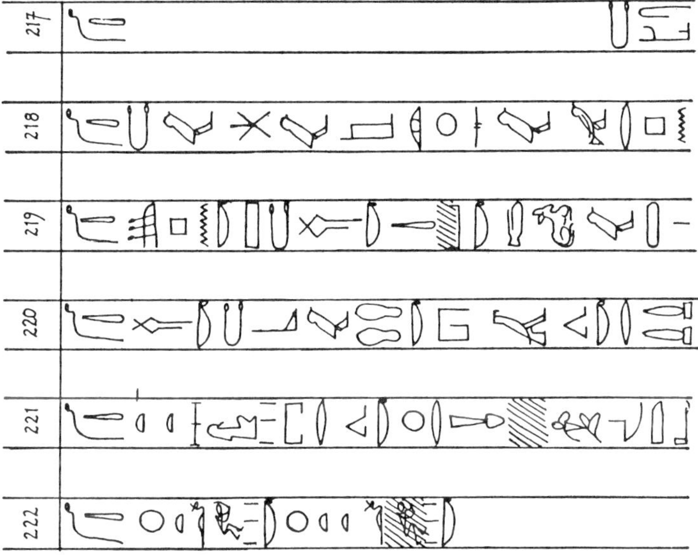

Figure 54. Hand copy, west wall, Register A, lines 217–222.

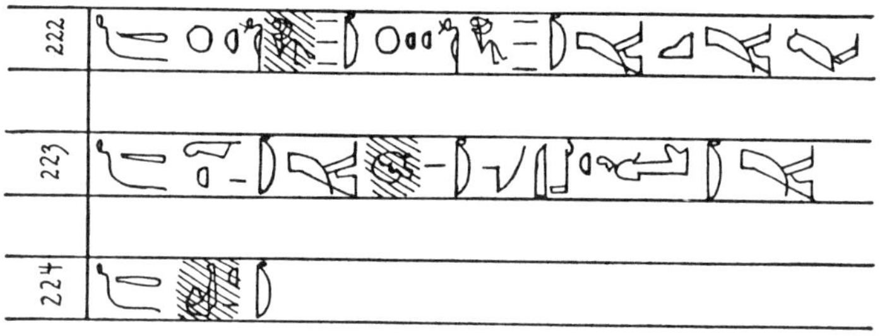

The Tomb Chamber of Ḥsw The Elder

Figure 55. Hand copy, west wall, Register A, lines 222–224.

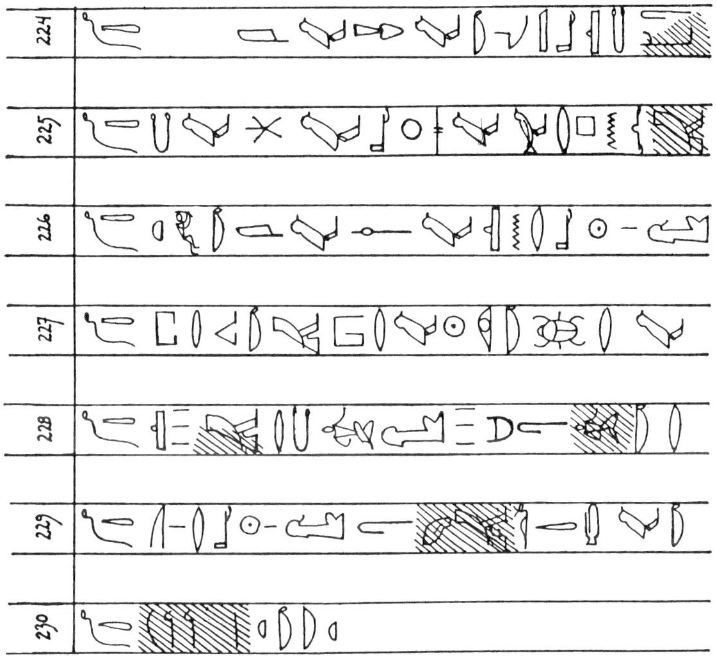

Figure 56. Hand copy, west wall, Register A, lines 224–230.

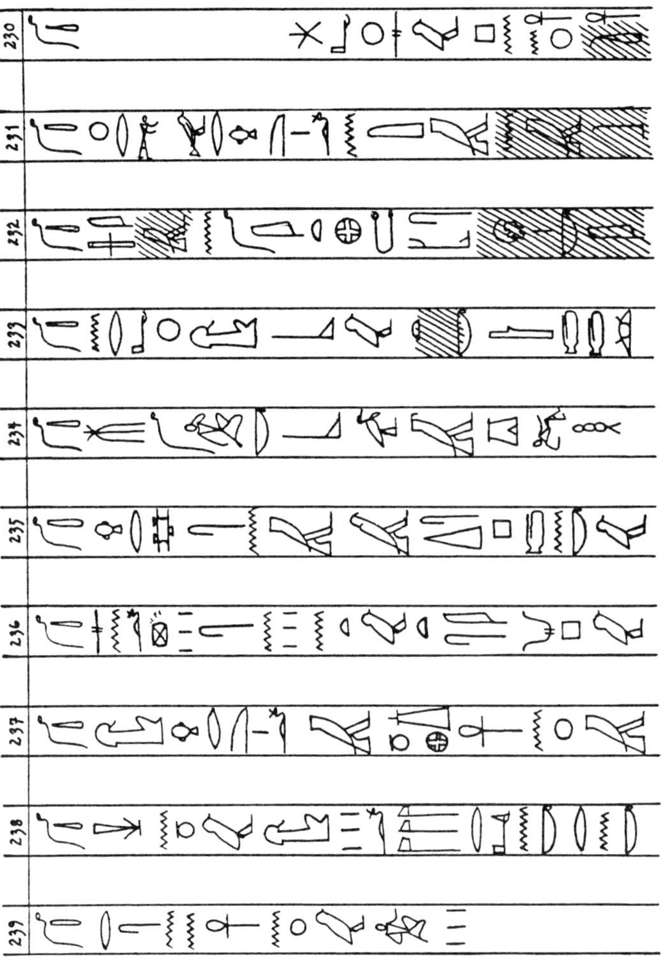

Figure 57. Hand copy, west wall, Register A, lines 230–239.

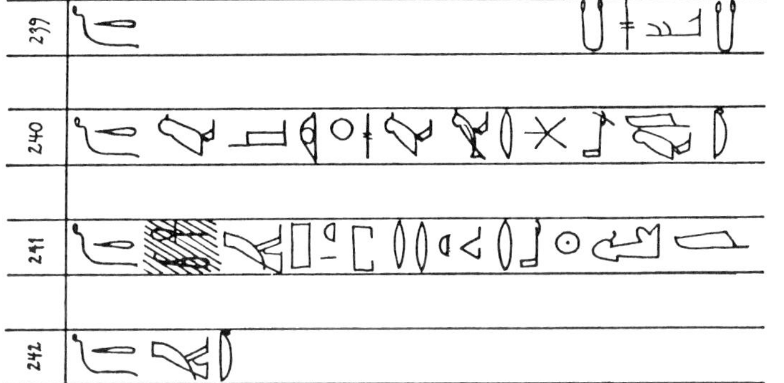

Figure 58. Hand copy, west wall, Register A, lines 239–242.

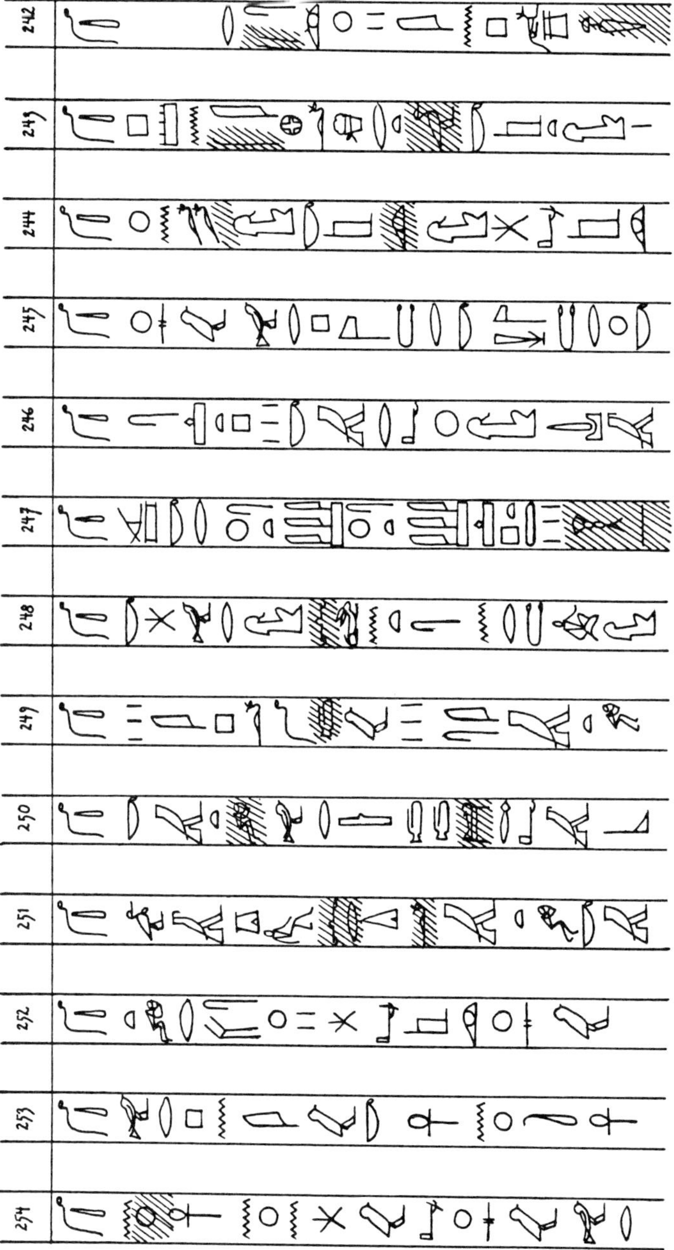

Figure 59. Hand copy, west wall, Register A, lines 242–254.

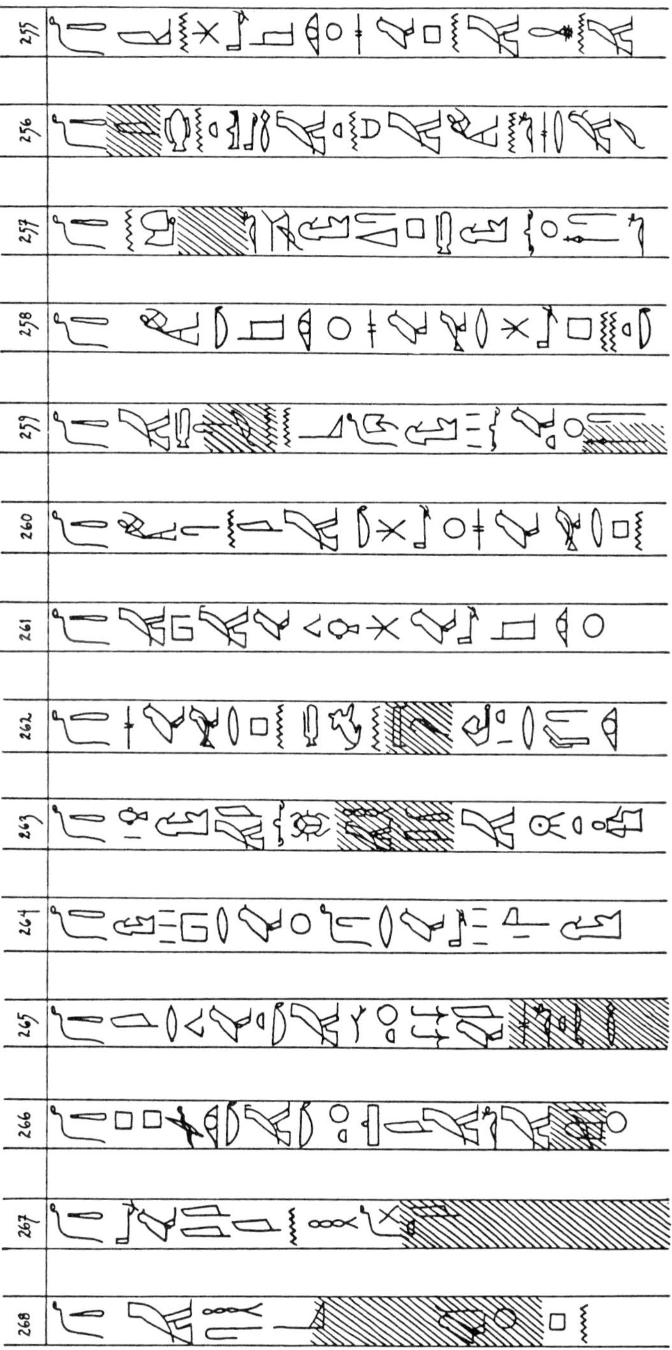

Figure 60. Hand copy, west wall, Register B, lines 255–268.

The Tomb Chamber of Ḥsw The Elder

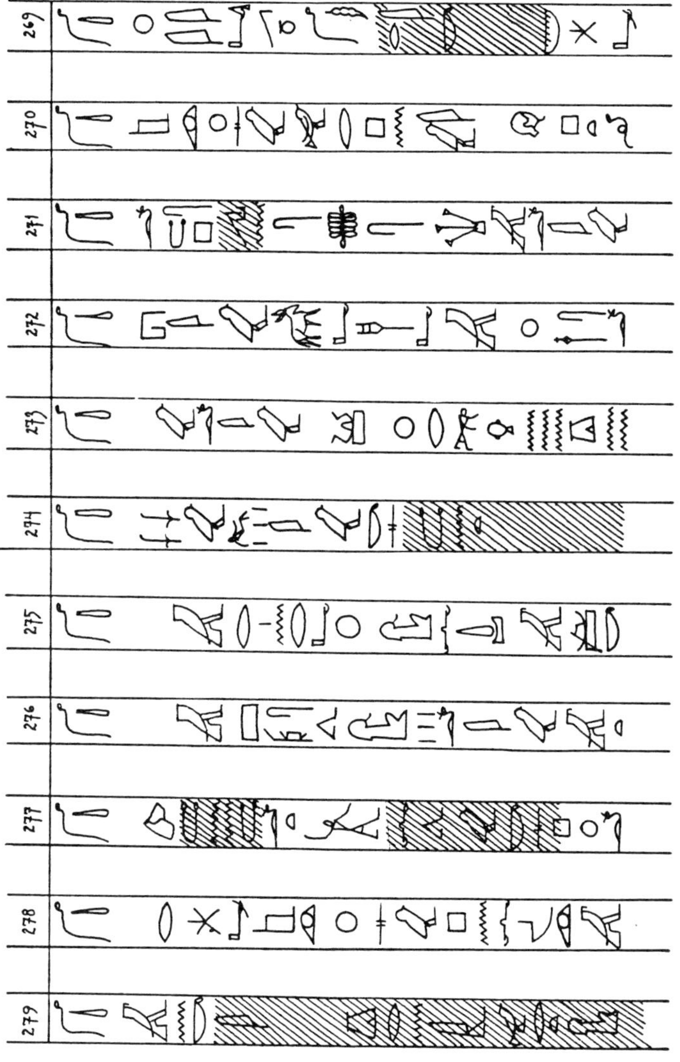

Figure 61. Hand copy, west wall, Register B, lines 269–279.

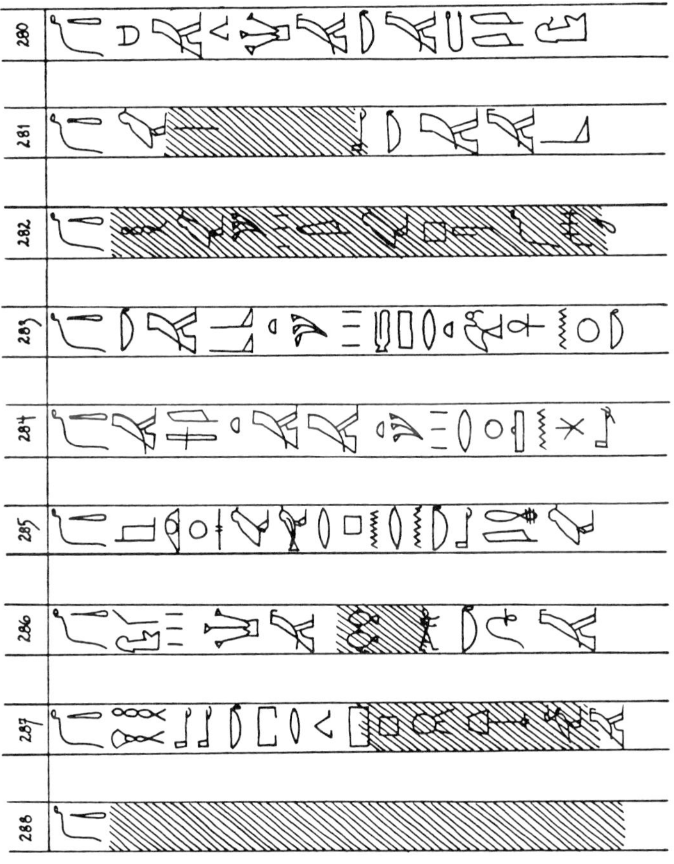

Figure 62. Hand copy, west wall, Register B, lines 280–288.

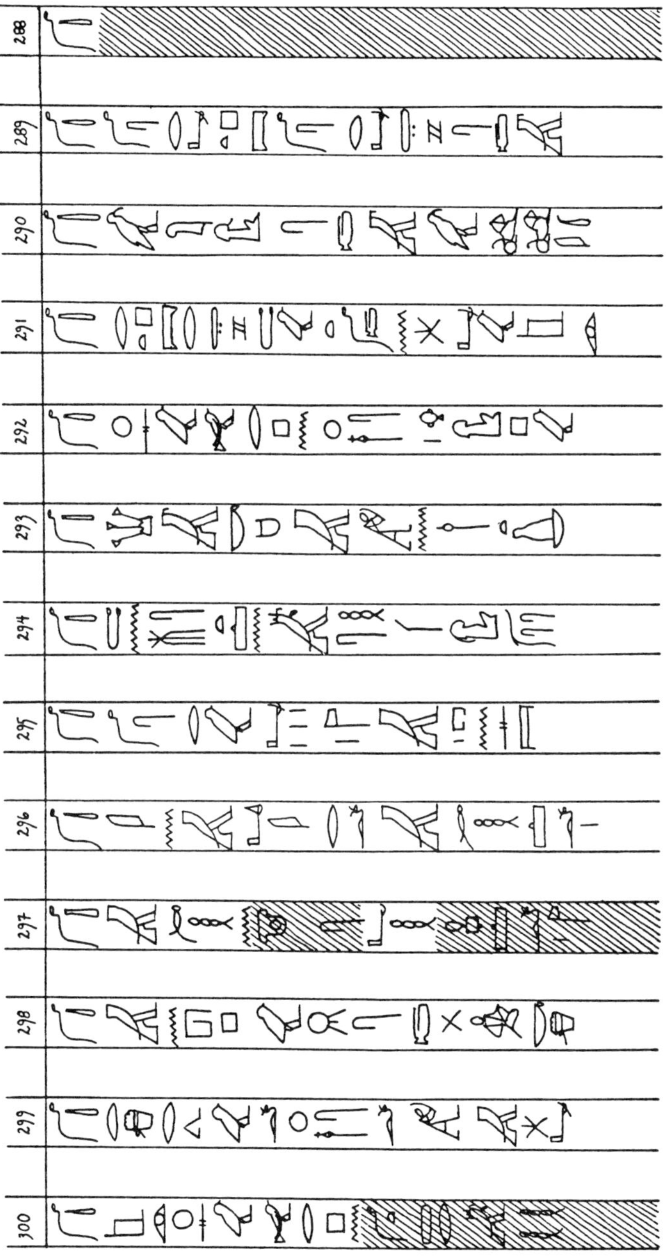

Figure 63. Hand copy, west wall, Register B, lines 288–300.

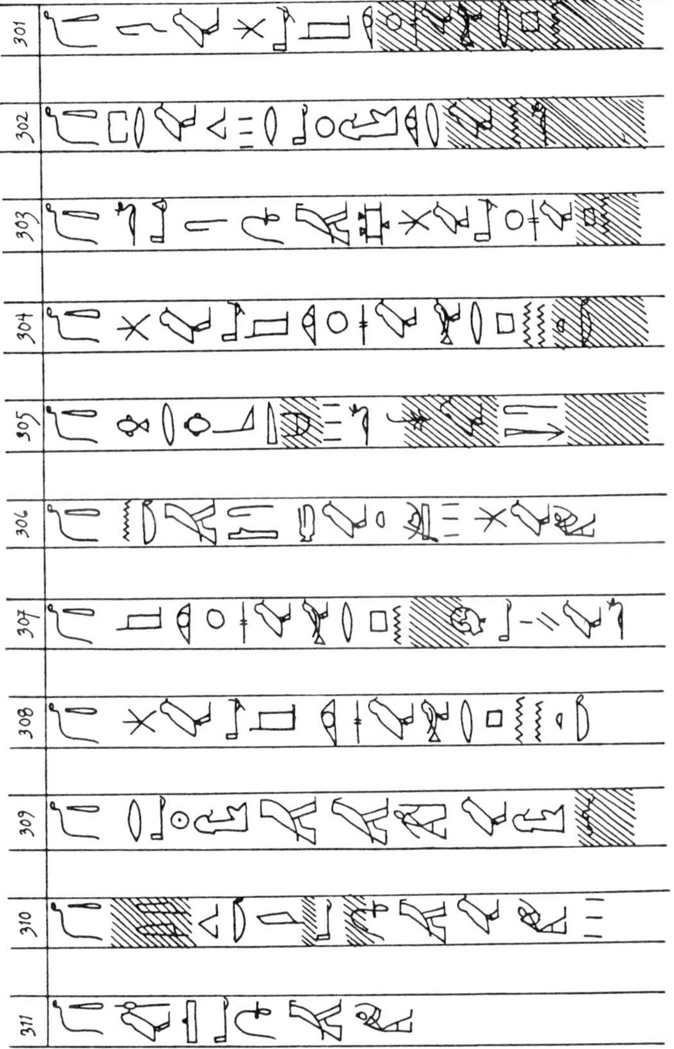

Figure 64. Hand copy, west wall, Register B, lines 301–311.

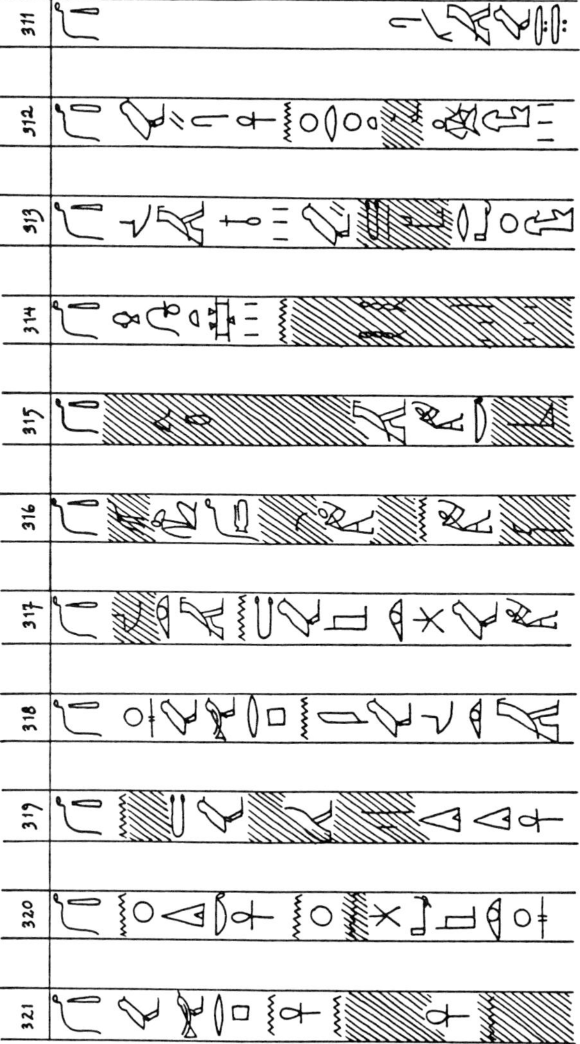

Figure 65. Hand copy, west wall, Register B, lines 311–321.

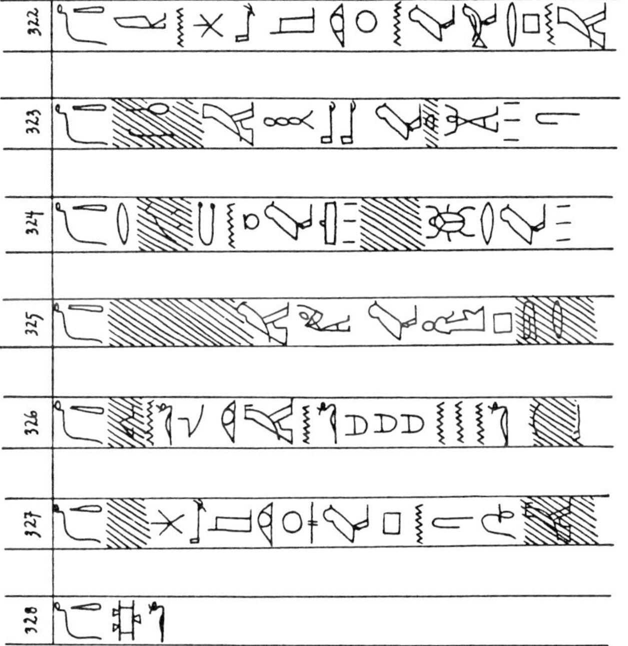

Figure 66. Hand copy, west wall, Register B, lines 322–328.

Figure 67. Hand copy, west wall, Register B, lines 328–342.

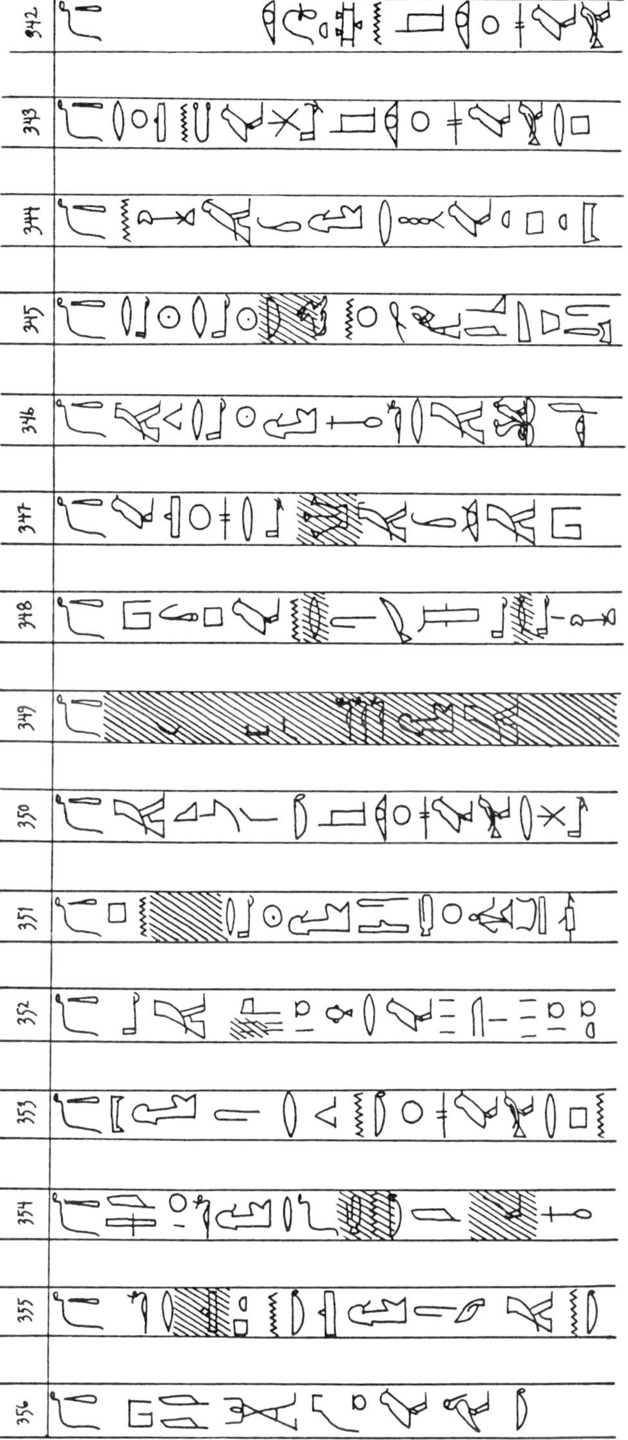

Figure 68. Hand copy, west wall, Register B, lines 342–356.

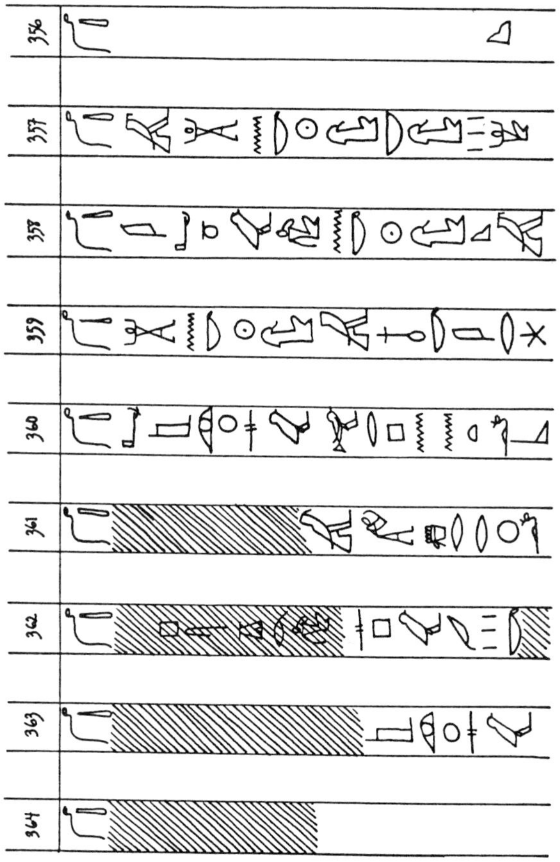

The Tomb Chamber of Ḥsw The Elder

Figure 69. Hand copy, west wall, Register B, lines 356–364.

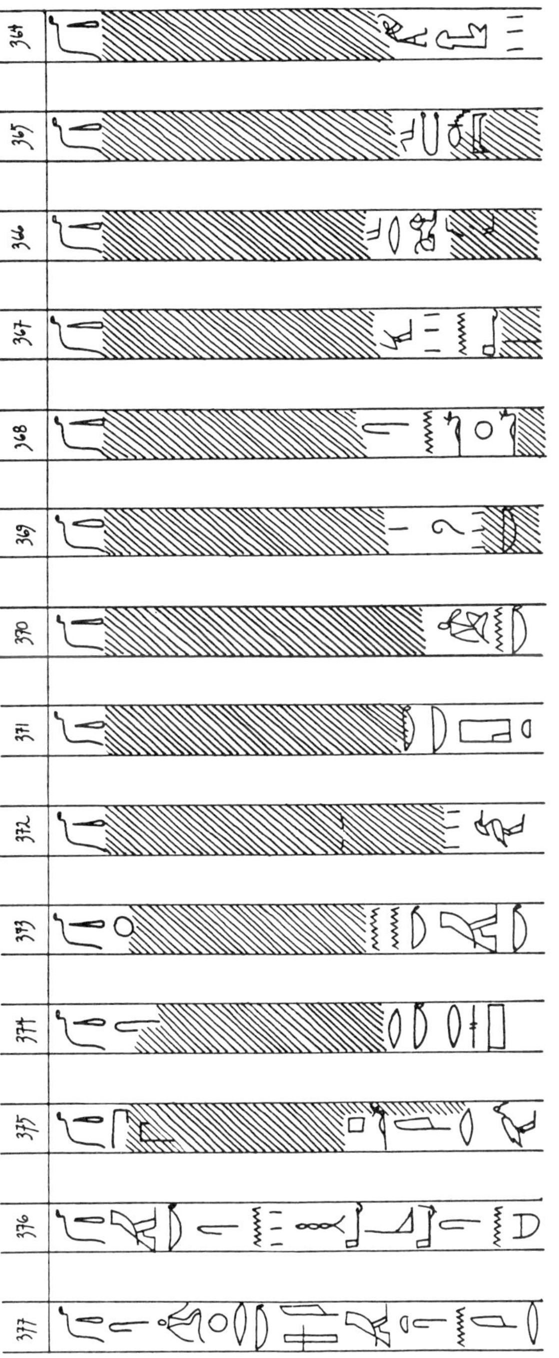

Figure 70. Hand copy, west wall, Register B, lines 364–385 (continued on figure 71).

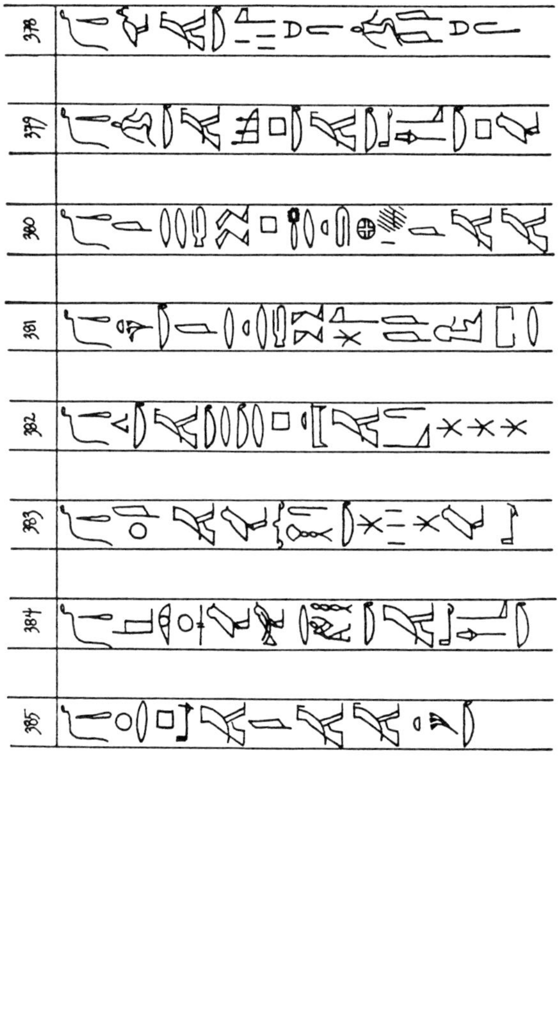

Figure 71. Hand copy, west wall, Register B, lines 364–385 (continued from figure 70).

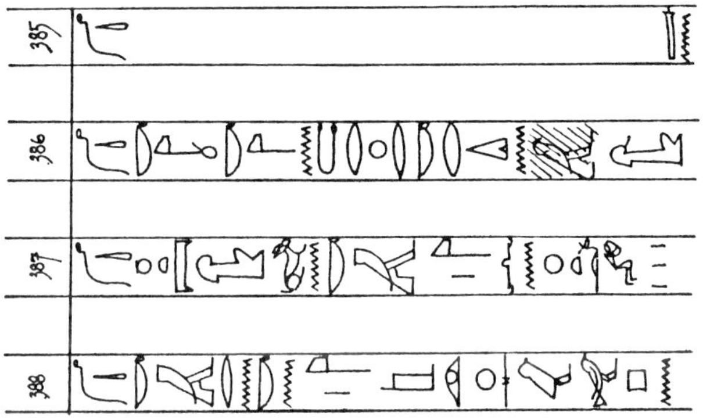

Figure 72. Hand copy, west wall, Register B, lines 385–388.

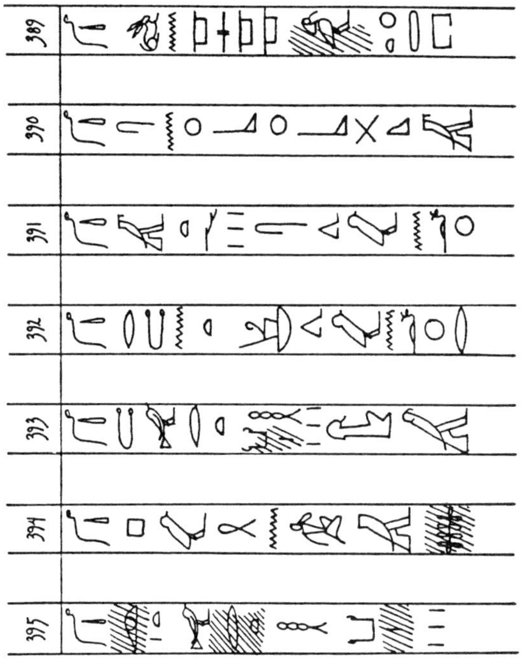

Figure 73. Hand copy, west wall, Register C, lines 389–395.

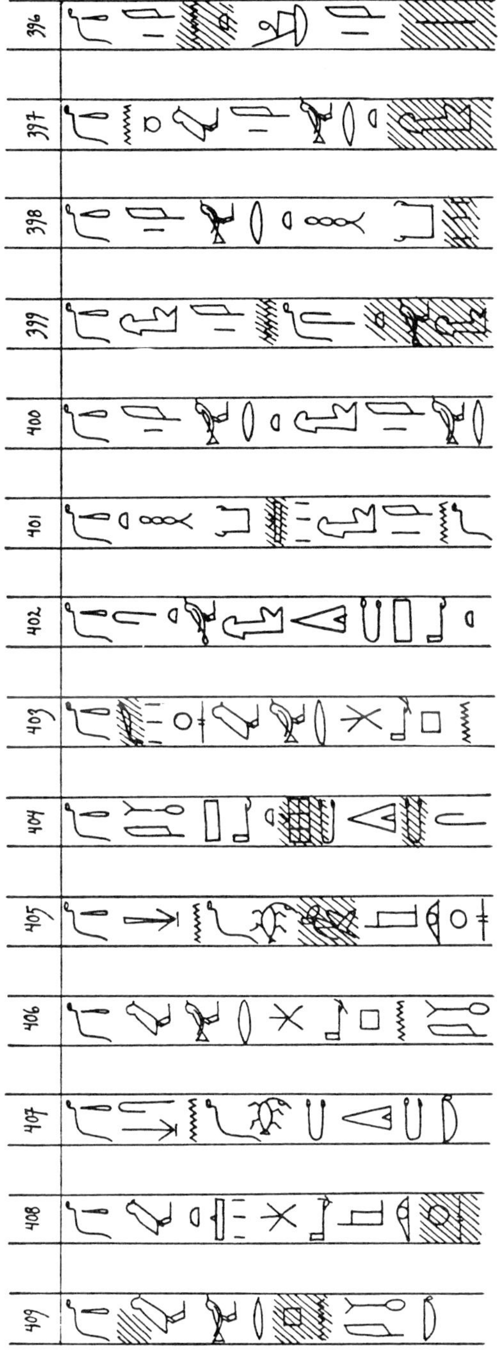

Figure 74. Hand copy, west wall, Register C, lines 396–428 (continued on figures 75 and 76).

The Tomb Chamber of Ḥsw The Elder

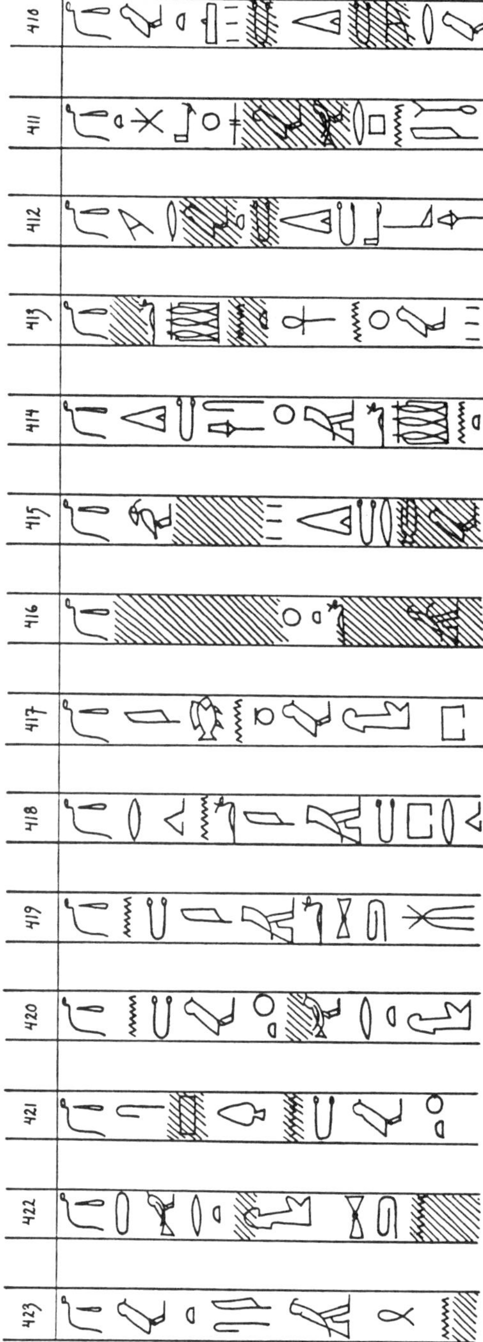

Figure 75. Hand copy, west wall, Register C, lines 396–428 (continued from figure 74; continued on figure 76).

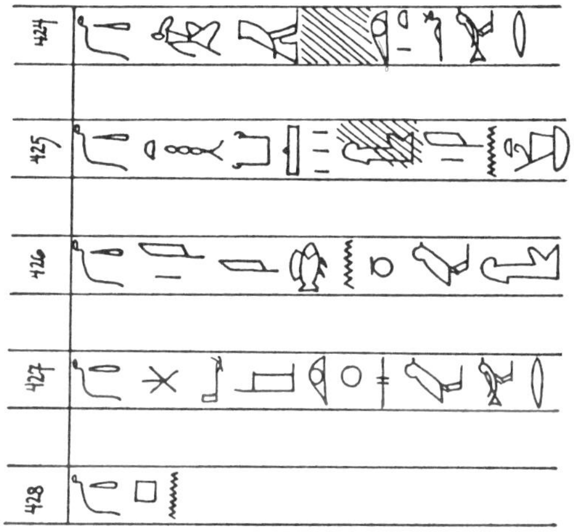

Figure 76. Hand copy, west wall, Register C, lines 396–428 (continued from figures 74 and 75).

The Tomb Chamber of Ḥsw The Elder

Figure 77. Hand copy, west wall, Register C, lines 427–499 (continued on figures 78–82).

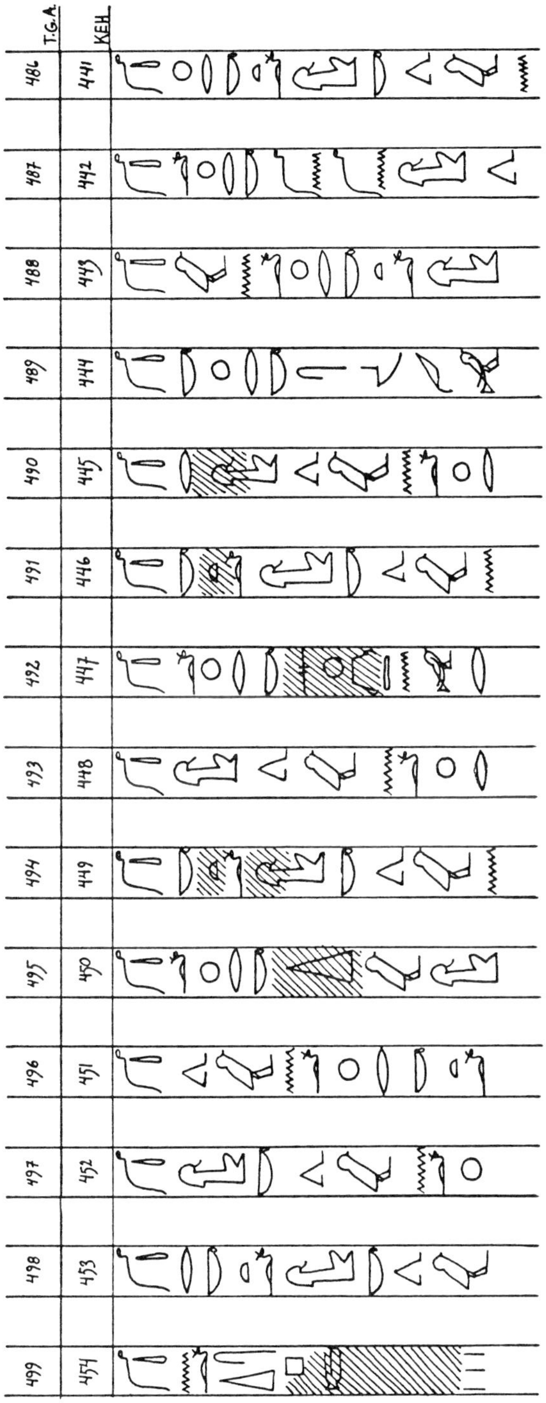

Figure 78. Hand copy, west wall, Register C, lines 427–499 (continued from figure 77; continued on figures 79–82).

The Tomb Chamber of Ḥsw The Elder

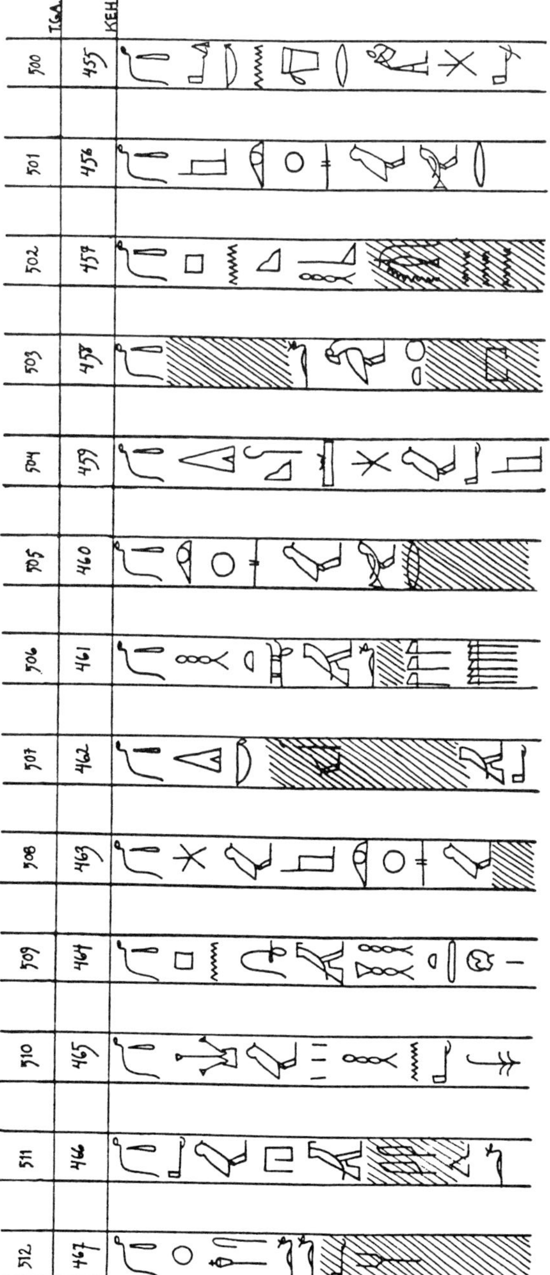

Figure 79. Hand copy, west wall, Register C, lines 427–499 (continued from figure 78; continued on figures 80–82).

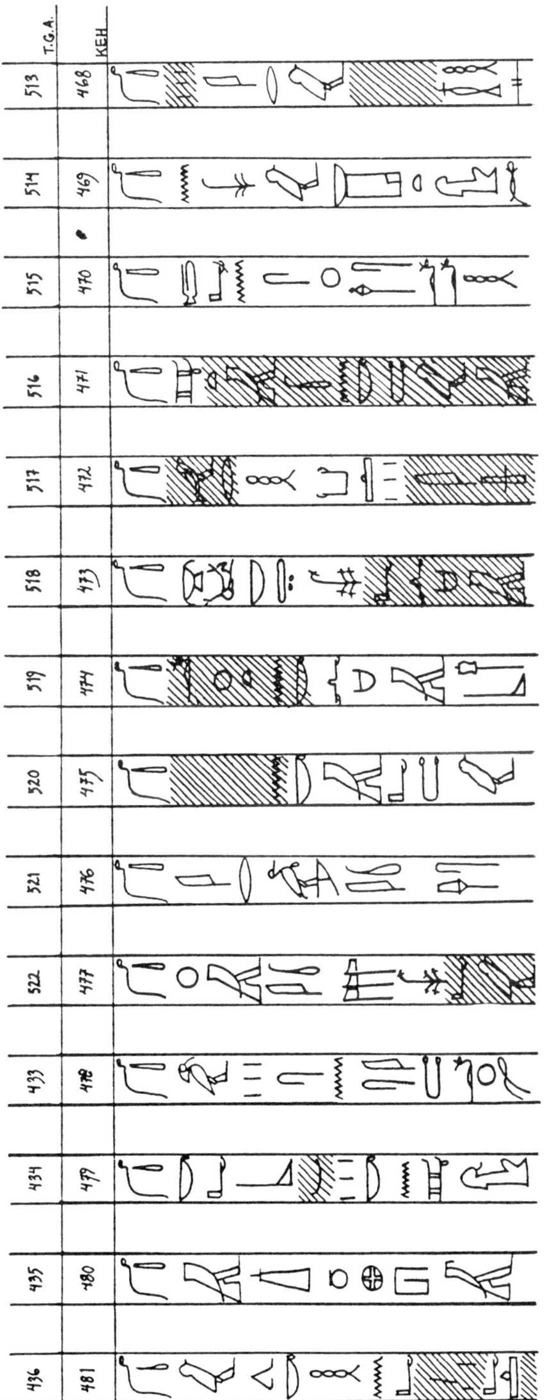

Figure 80. Hand copy, west wall, Register C, lines 427–499 (continued from figure 79; continued on figures 81 and 82).

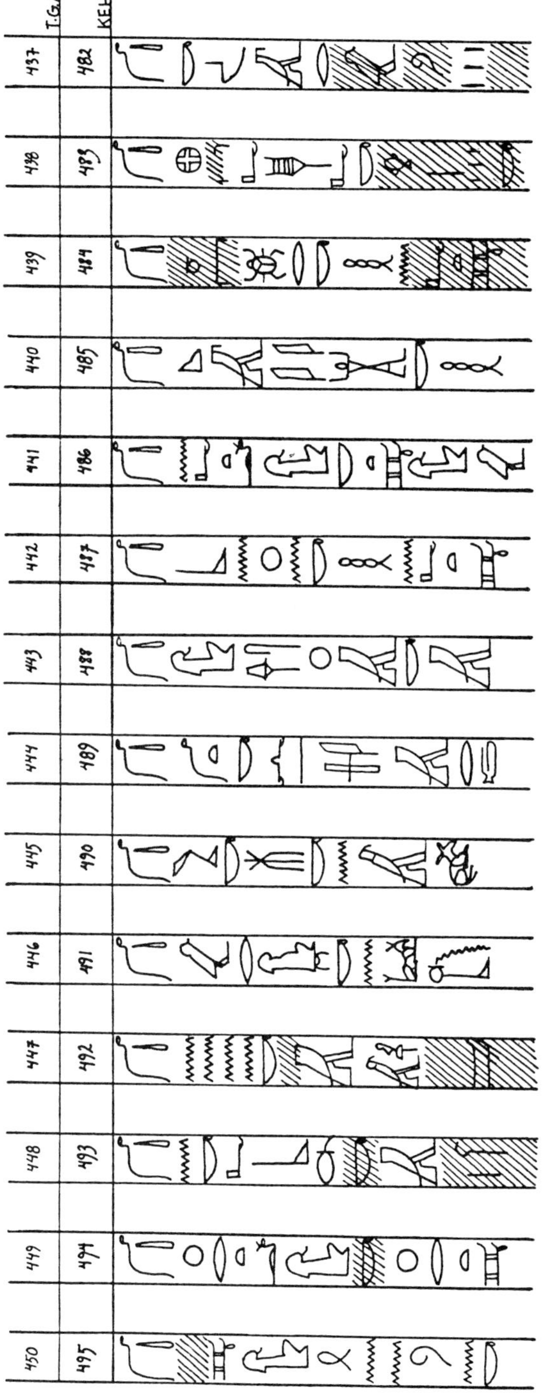

The Tomb Chamber of Ḥsw The Elder

Figure 81. Hand copy, west wall, Register C, lines 427–499 (continued from figure 80; continued on figure 82).

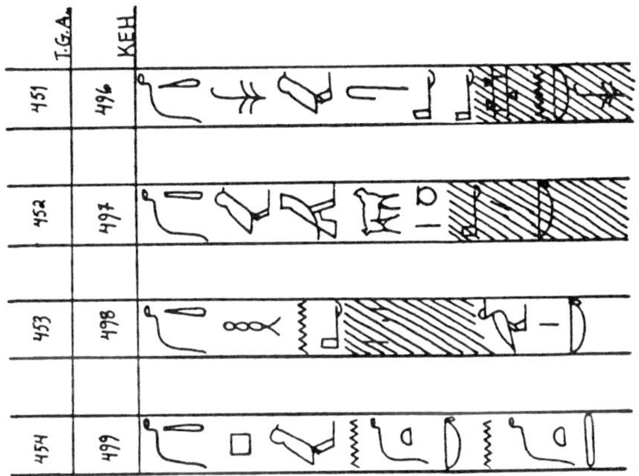

Figure 82. Hand copy, west wall, Register C, lines 427–499 (continued from figure 81).

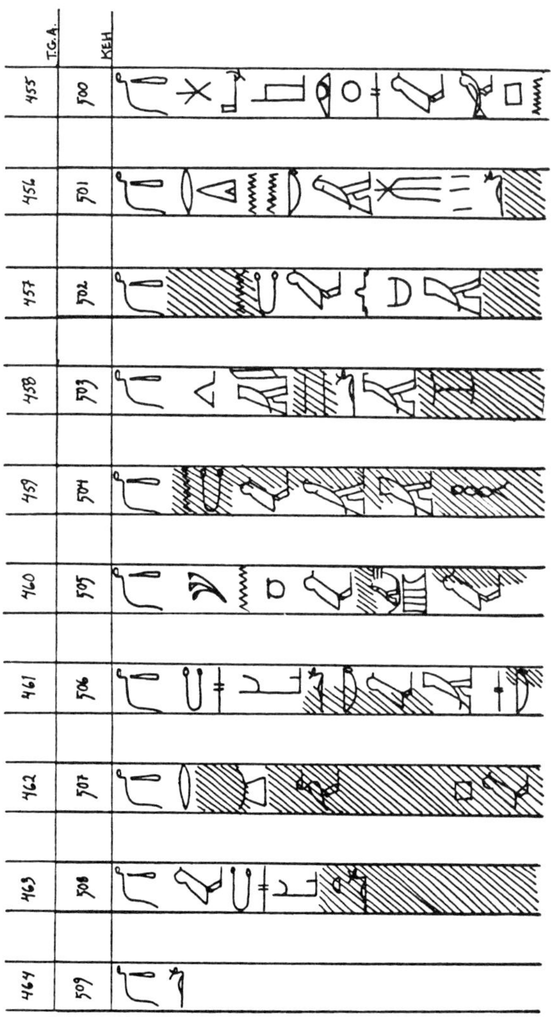

Figure 83. Hand copy, west wall, Register C, lines 500–599.

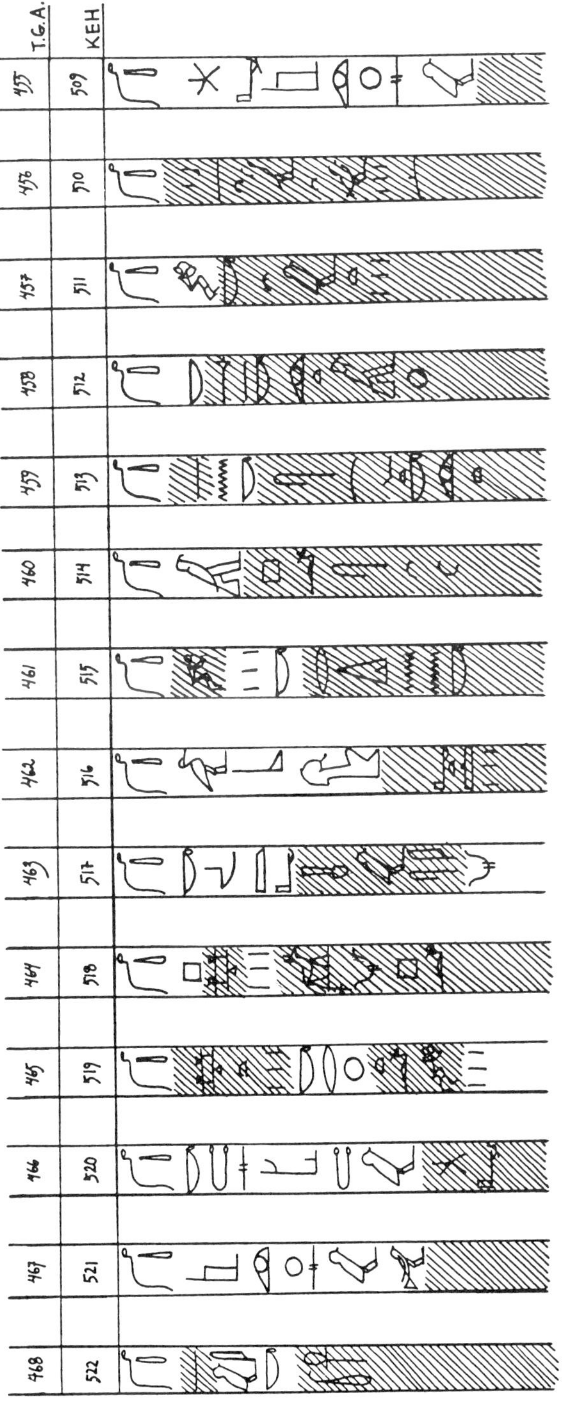

Figure 84. Hand copy, west wall, Register C, lines 509–522.

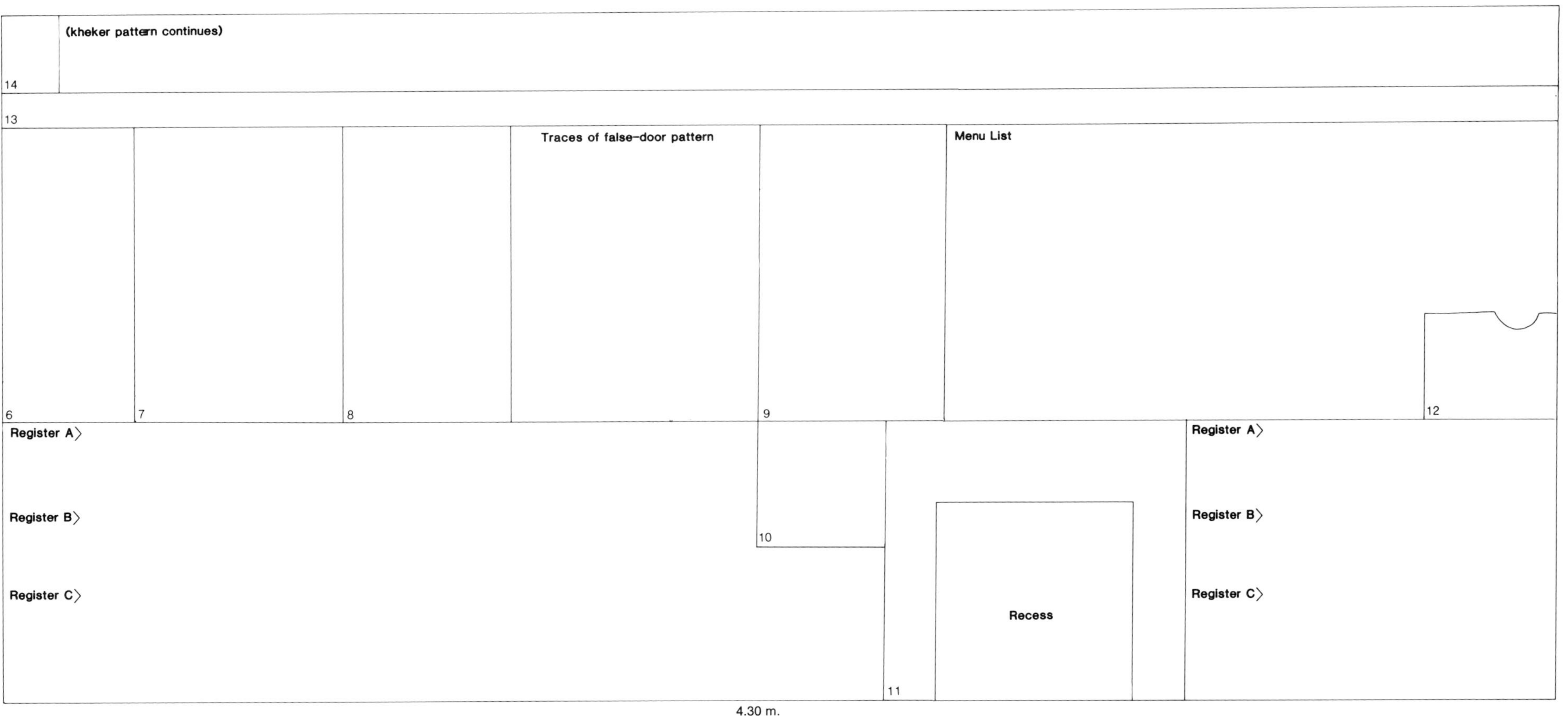

Figure 85. Diagram of the east wall of the tomb chamber.

Figure 86a–b. Photographs, upper third of the relief, east wall.

Figure 86c–e. Photographs, upper third of the relief, east wall.

a.

b.

c.

Figure 87a–c. Photographs, middle third of the relief, east wall.

Figure 87d–e. Photographs, middle third of the relief, east wall.

Figure 88. Composite drawing of the relief, east wall.

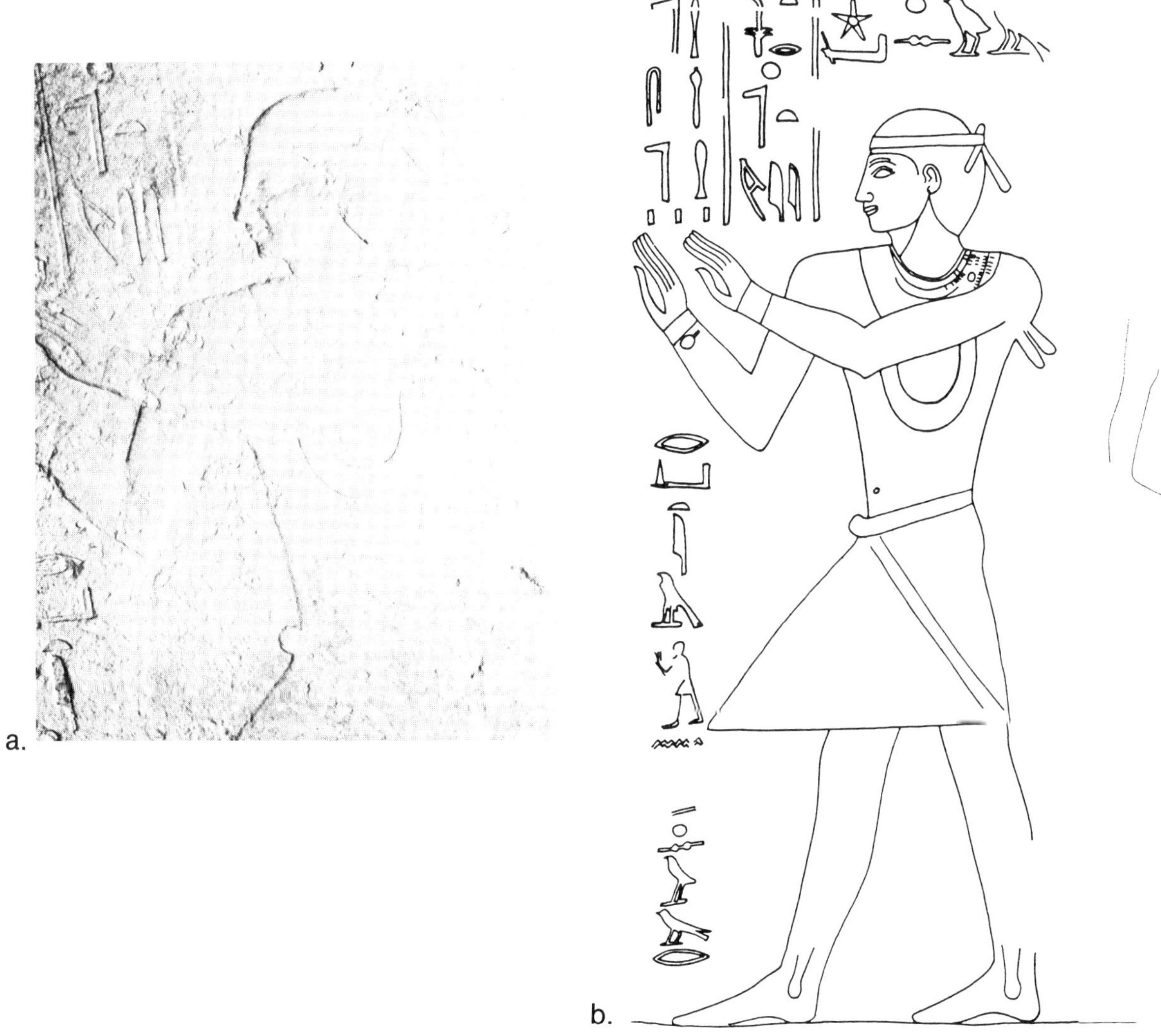

Figure 89a–b. Photograph and drawing, *Ḥsw*, north end of the relief, east wall.

Figure 90a–b. Photograph and drawing, offering bearers, north end of the relief, east wall.

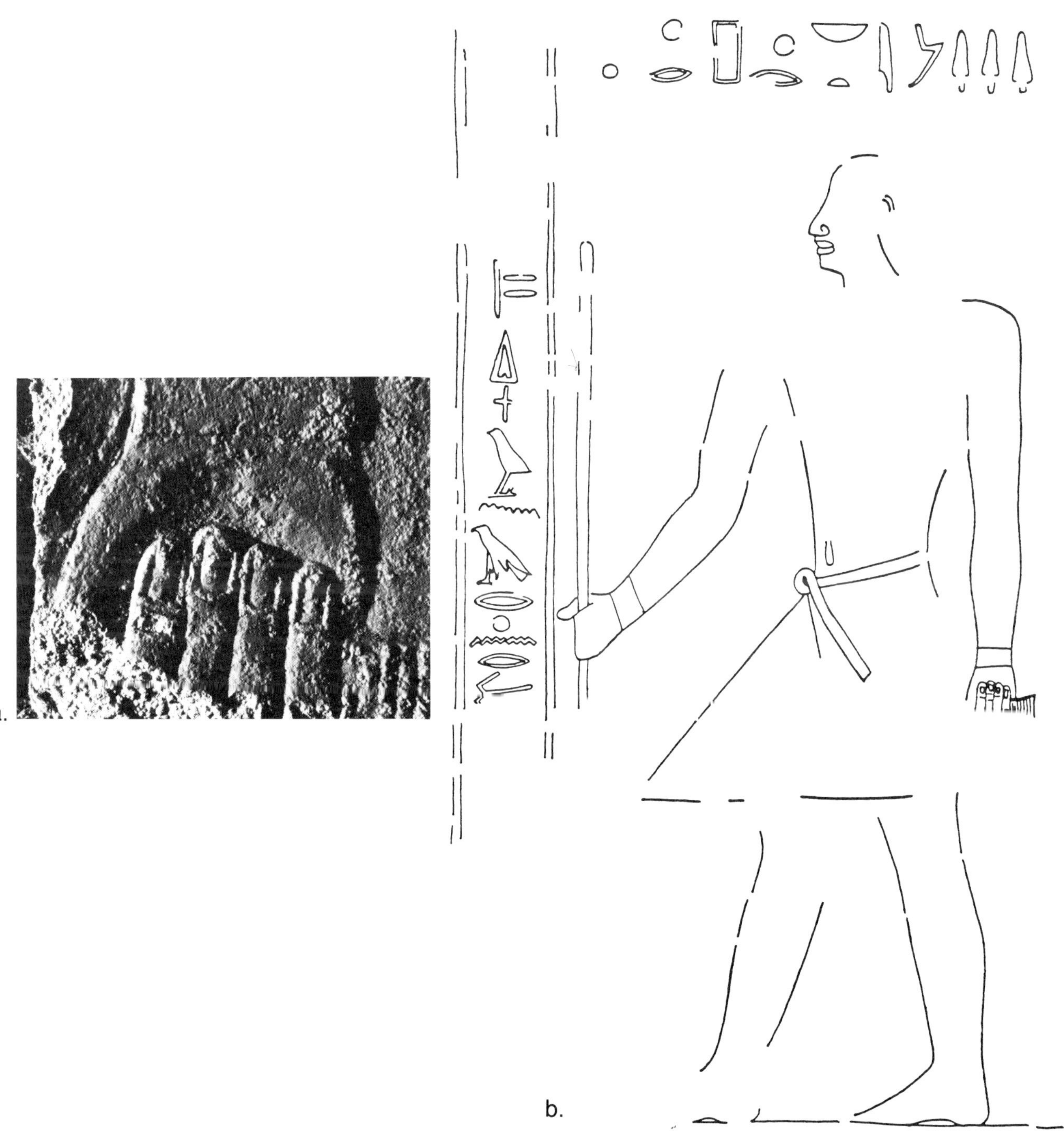

Figure 91a–b. Photograph and drawing, *Ḥsw*, relief, east wall.

Figure 92a–b. Photographs, offering table, middle portion of the relief, east wall.

Figure 93. Drawings, offering table, middle portion of the relief, east wall.

Figure 94. Photograph, menu of funerary offerings, middle to south portion of the relief, east wall. Courtesy of the Oriental Institute.

Figure 95. Photograph, menu of funerary oﬀerings, middle to south portion of the relief, east wall. Courtesy of the Oriental Institute.

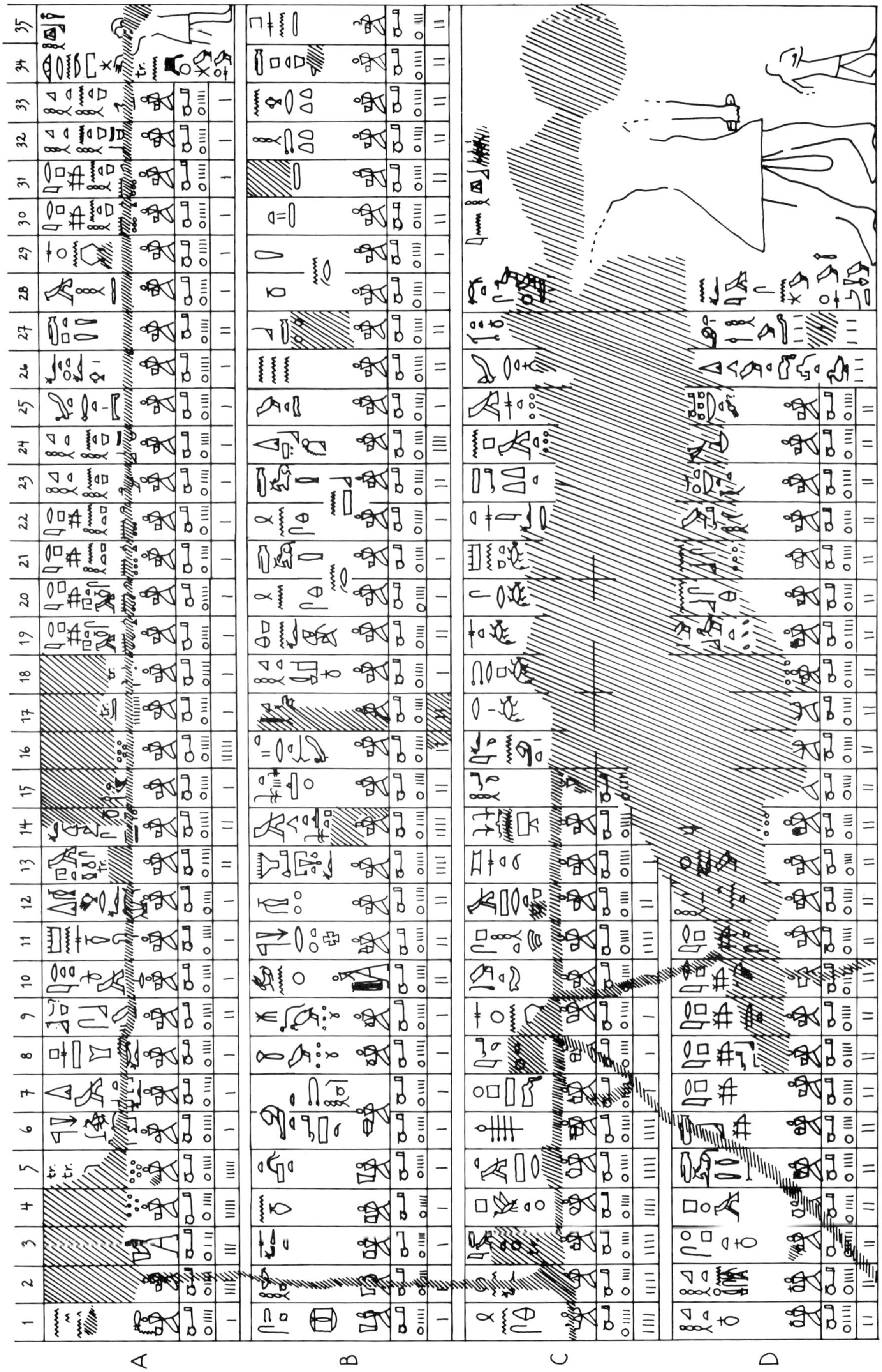

The Tomb Chamber of Ḥsw The Elder

Figure 96. Drawing, menu of funerary offerings, middle to south portion of the relief, east wall.

Figure 97a–c. Photographs, recess, lower third of the relief, east wall.

Figure 98. Drawing, recess, lower third of the relief, east wall.

Figure 99. Photograph of the funerary texts, north end of the east wall, showing Register A (top, lines 523–567), Register B (middle, lines 568–615), and Register C (bottom, lines 647–694). Courtesy of the Oriental Institute.

Figure 100. Photograph of the funerary texts, middle of the east wall, showing Register A (top, lines 553–567), Register B (middle, lines 598–646), and Register C (bottom, lines 677–724). Courtesy of the Oriental Institute.

Figure 101. Photograph of the funerary texts, south end of the east wall, showing Register A (top, lines 725–752, Register B (middle, lines 753–780), and Register C (bottom, lines 781–808). Courtesy of the Oriental Institute.

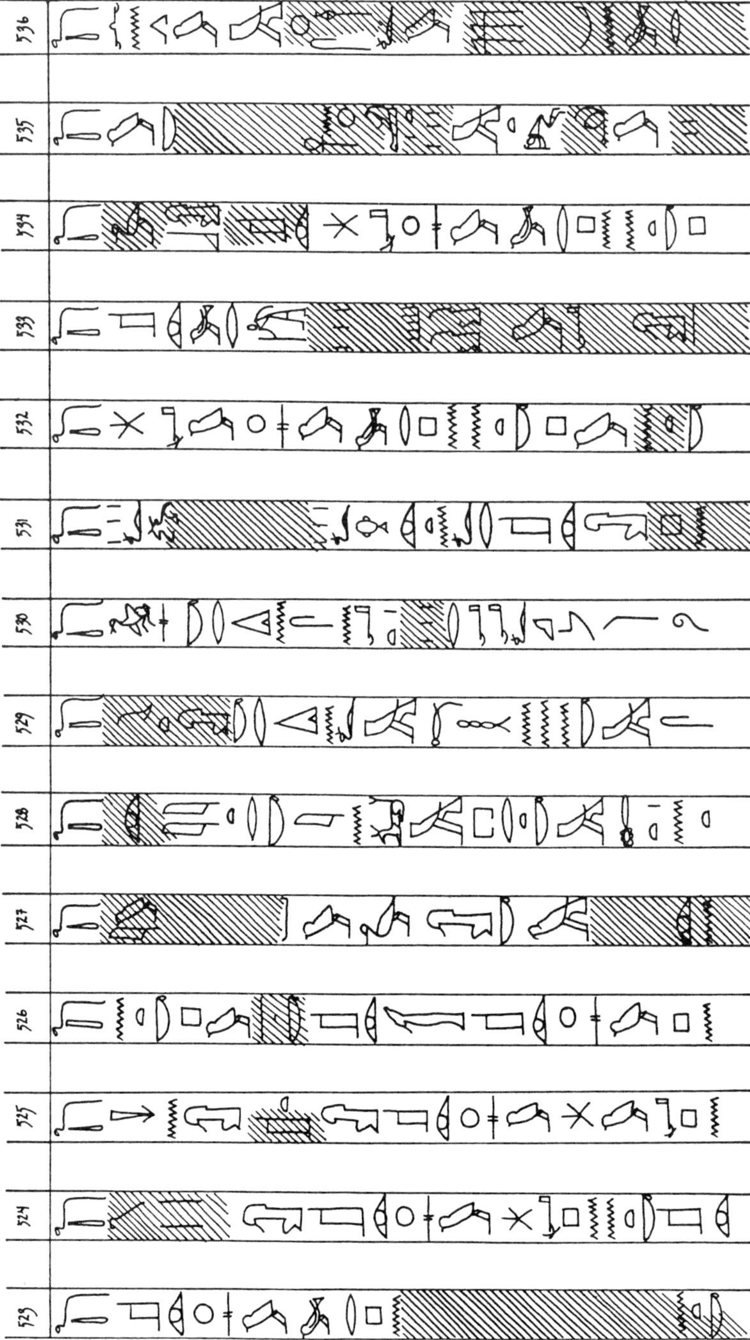

Figure 102. Hand copy, east wall, north end, Register A, lines 523–558 (continued on figures 103 and 104).

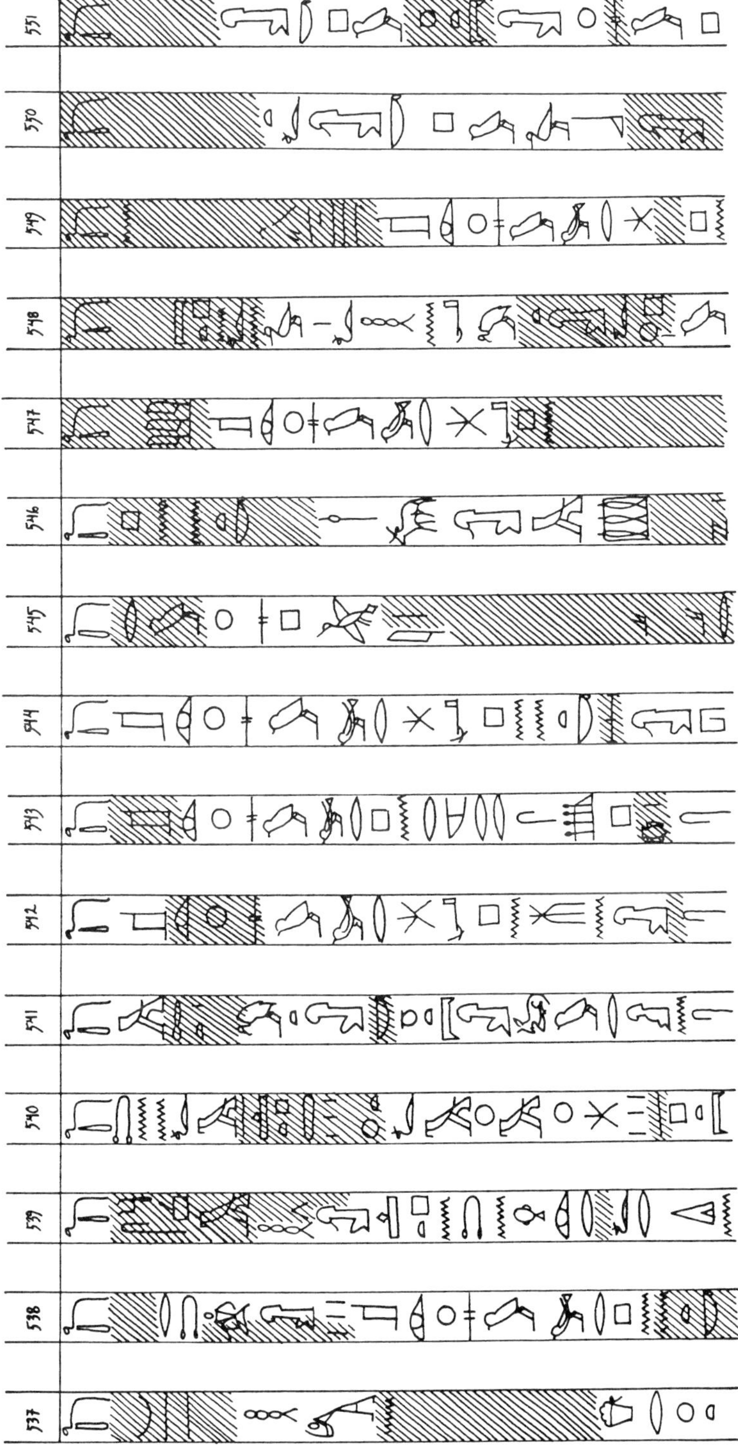

Figure 103. Hand copy, east wall, north end, Register A, lines 523–558 (continued from figure 102; continued on figure 104).

The Tomb Chamber of Ḥsw The Elder

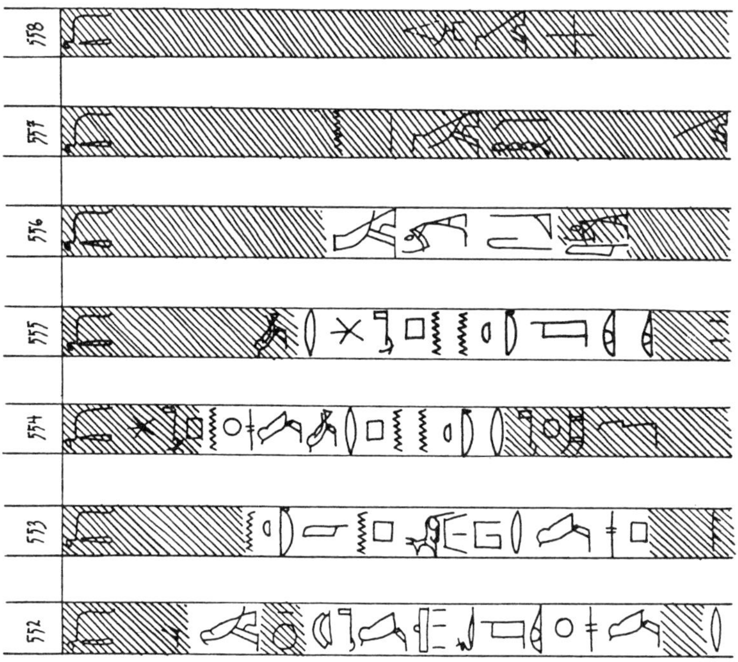

Figure 104. Hand copy, east wall, north end, Register A, lines 523–558 (continued from figure 103).

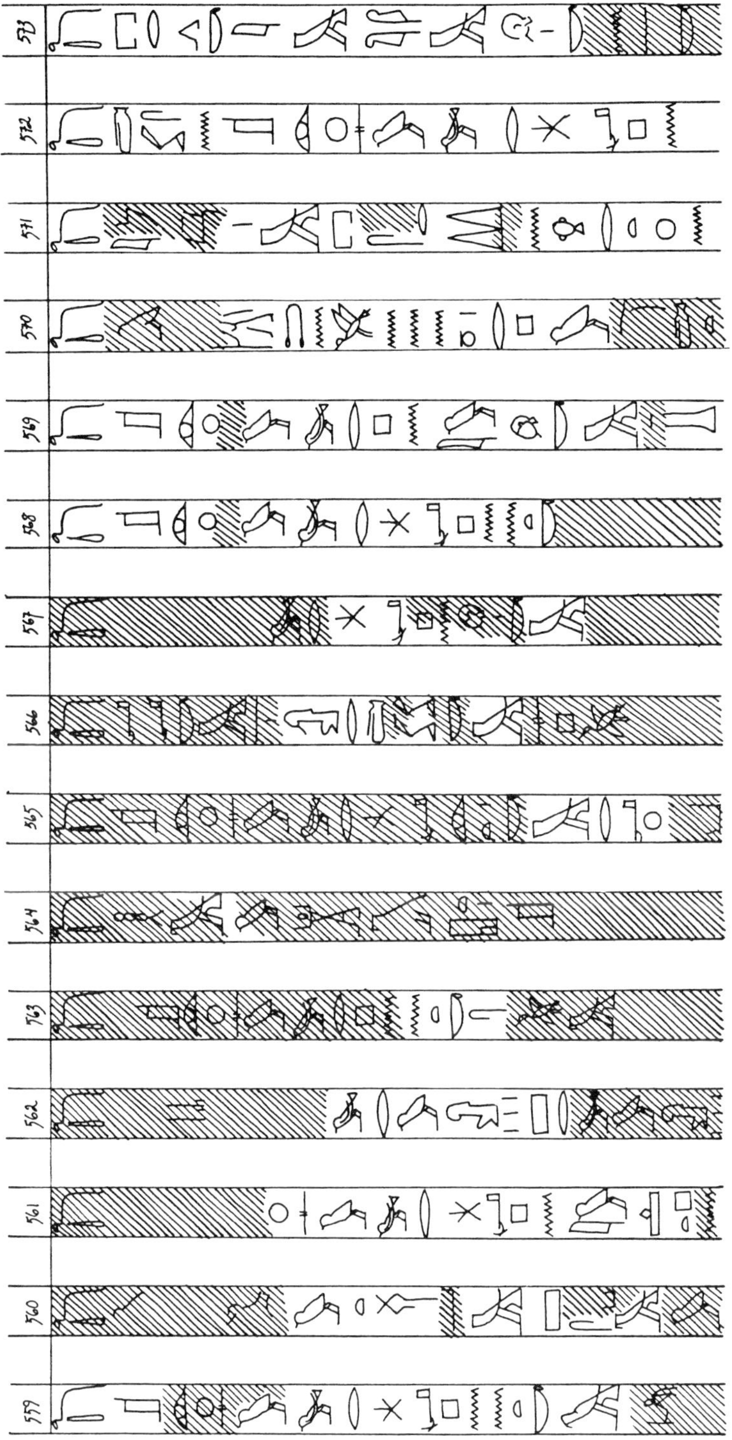

Figure 105. Hand copy, east wall, north end, Register A, lines 559–583 (continued on figure 106).

Figure 106. Hand copy, east wall, north end, Register B, lines 559–583 (continued from figure 105).

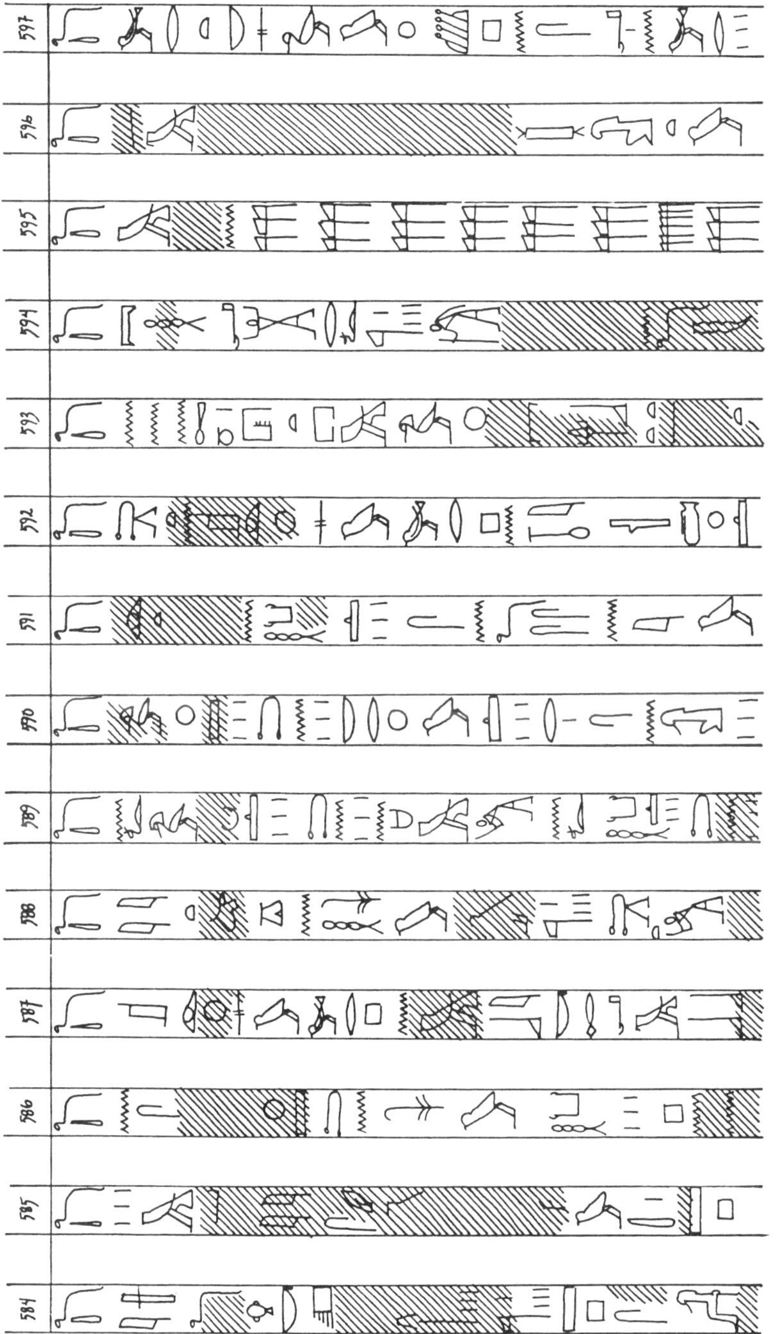

Figure 107. Hand copy, east wall, north end, Register B, lines 584–601 (continued on figure 108).

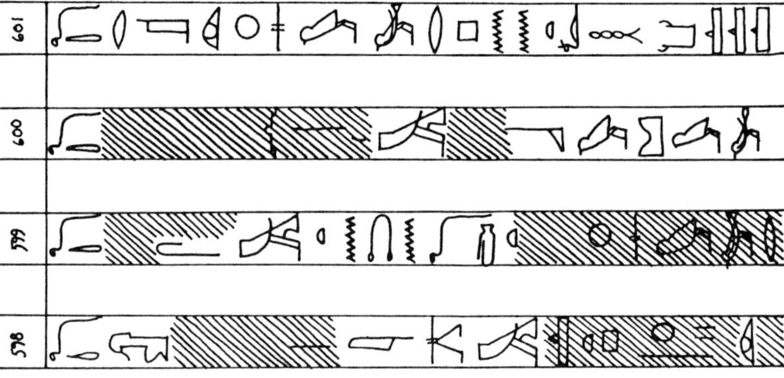

Figure 108. Hand copy, east wall, north end, Register B, lines 584–601 (continued from figure 107).

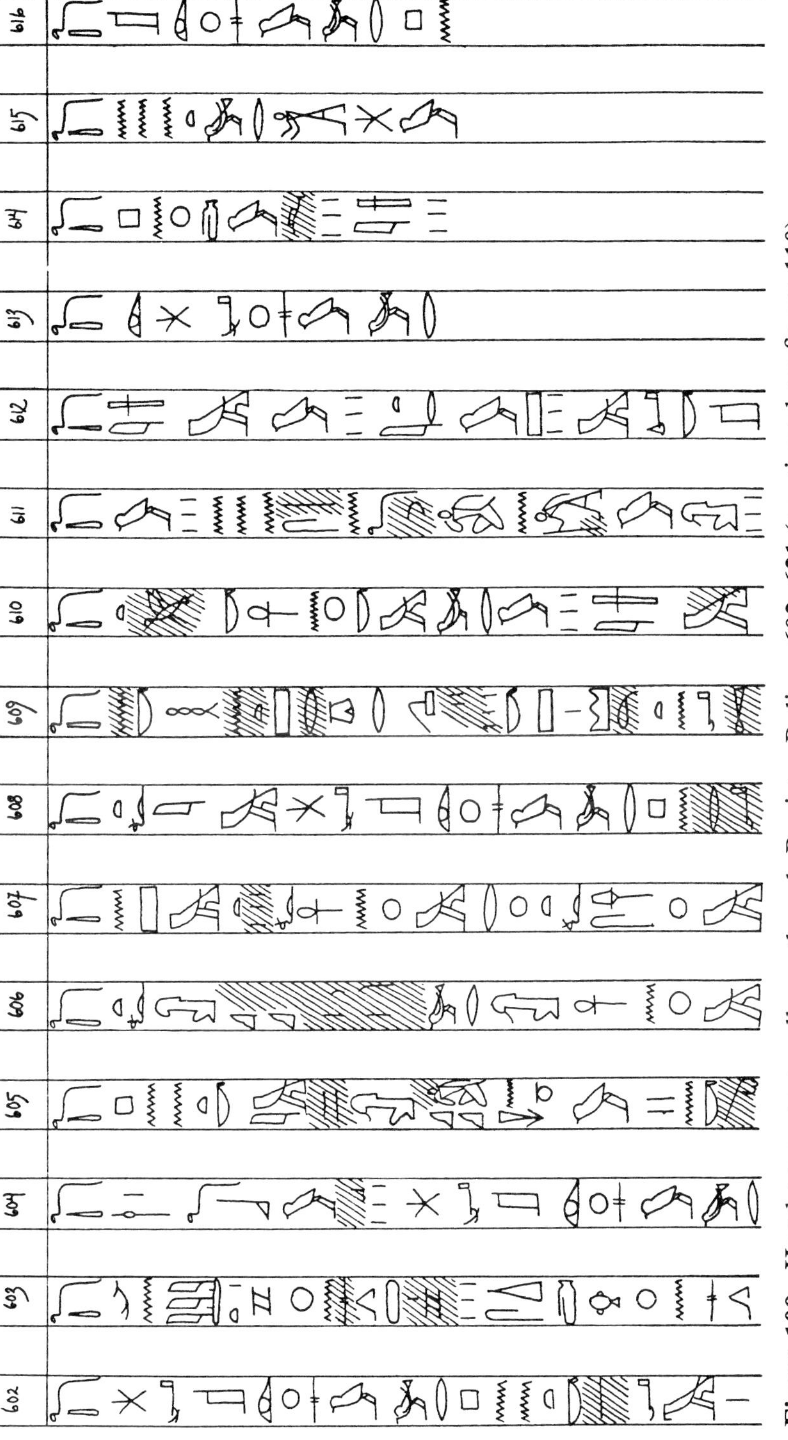

Figure 109. Hand copy, east wall, north end, Register B, lines 602–621 (continued on figure 110).

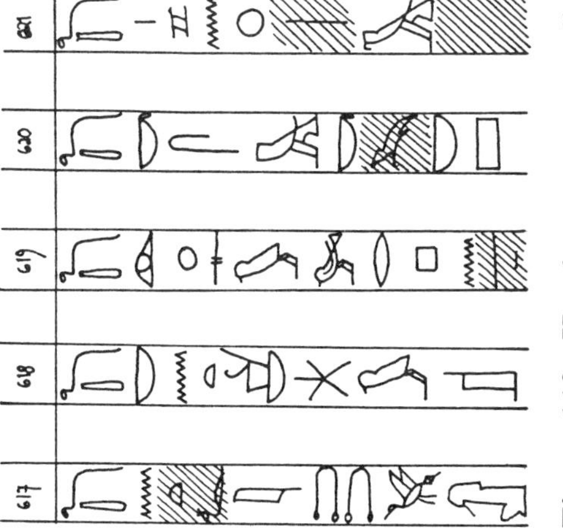

Figure 110. Hand copy, east wall, north end, Register B, lines 602–621 (continued from figure 109).

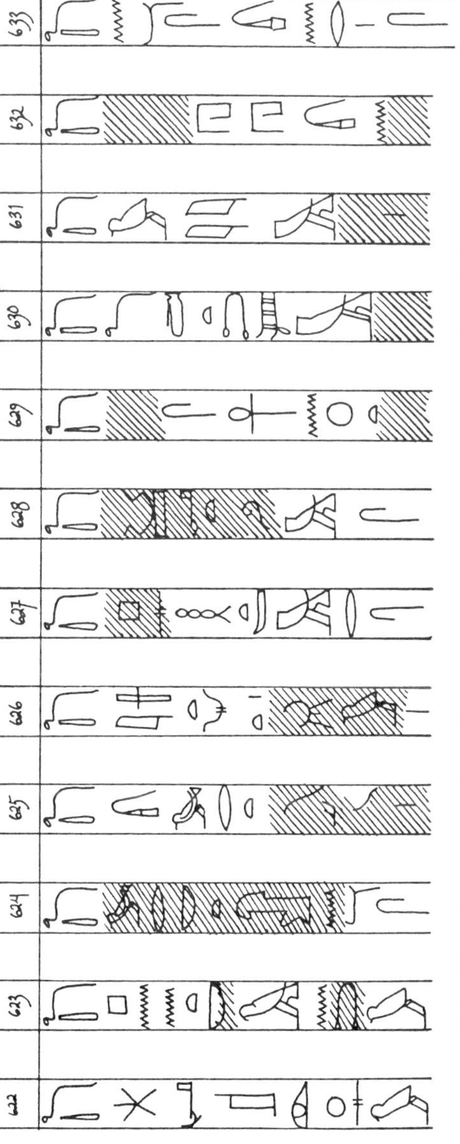

Figure 111. Hand copy, east wall, north end, Register B, lines 622–633.

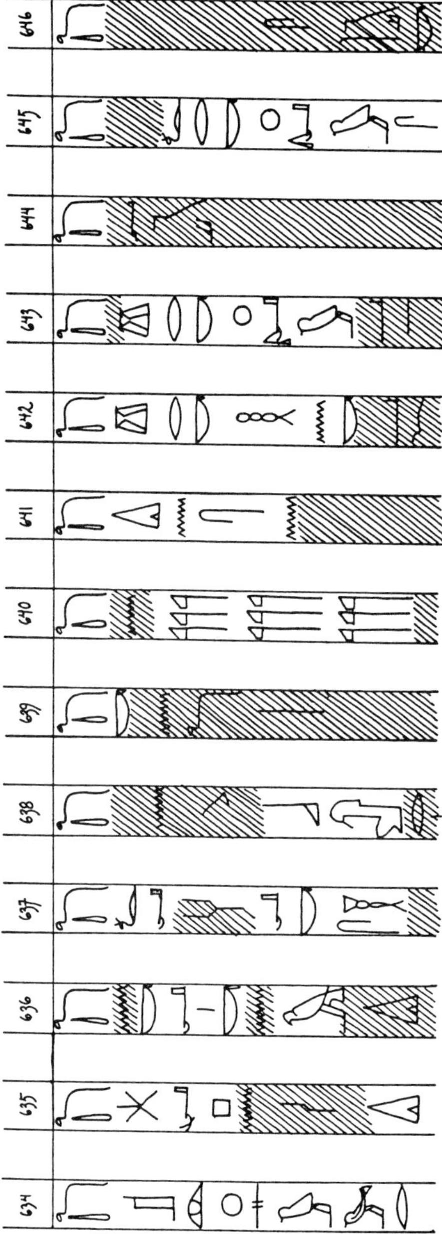

Figure 112. Hand copy, east wall, north end, Register B, lines 634–646.

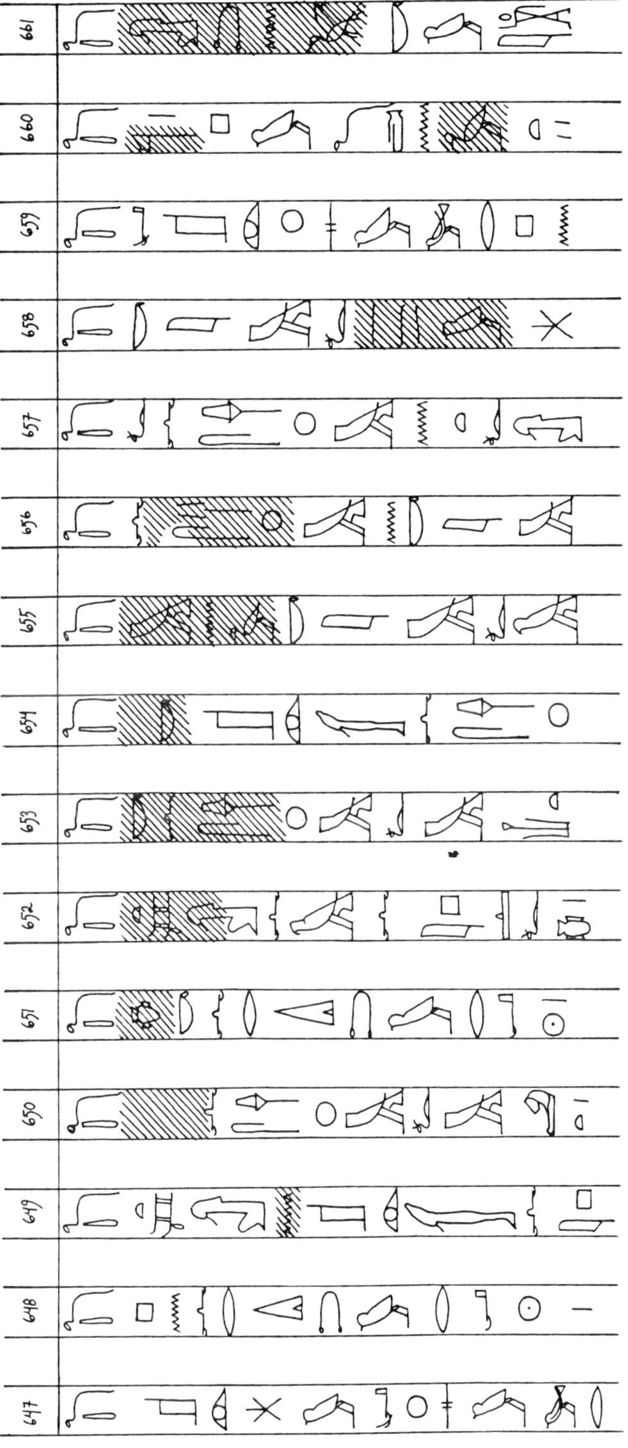

Figure 113. Hand copy, east wall, north end, Register C, lines 647–690 (continued on figures 114 and 115).

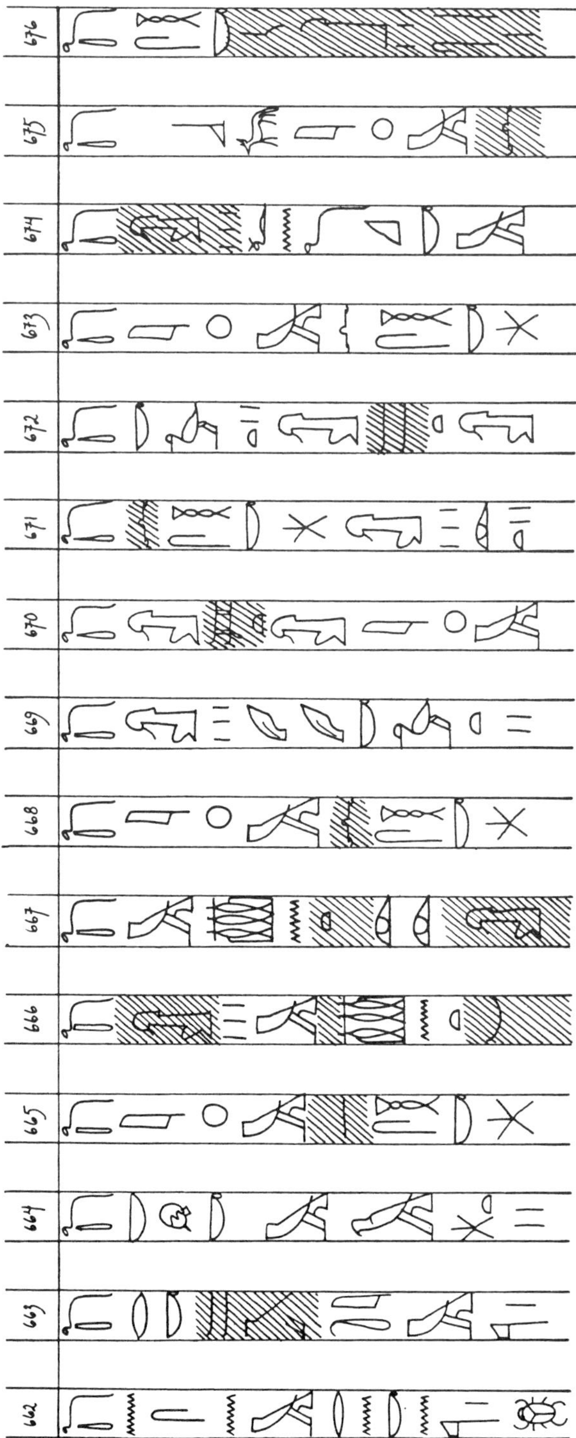

Figure 114. Hand copy, east wall, north end, Register C, lines 647–690 (continued from figure 113; continued on figure 115).

Figure 115. Hand copy, east wall, north end, Register C, lines 647–690 (continued from figure 114).

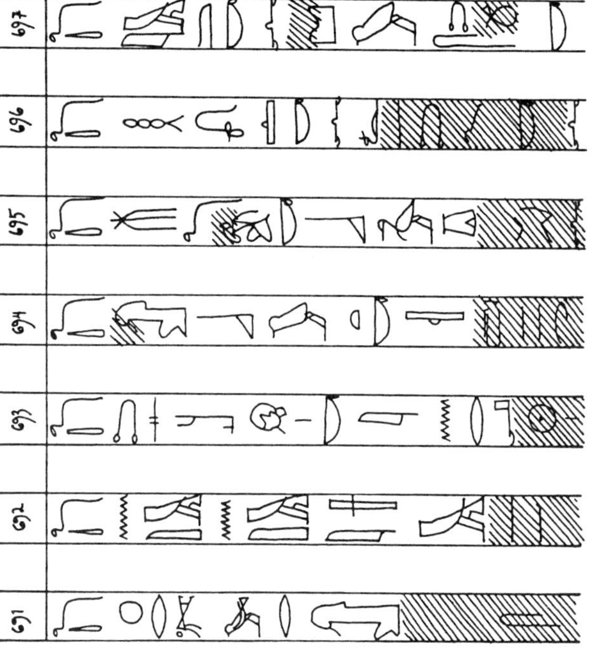

Figure 116. Hand copy, east wall, north end, Register C, lines 691–697(?).

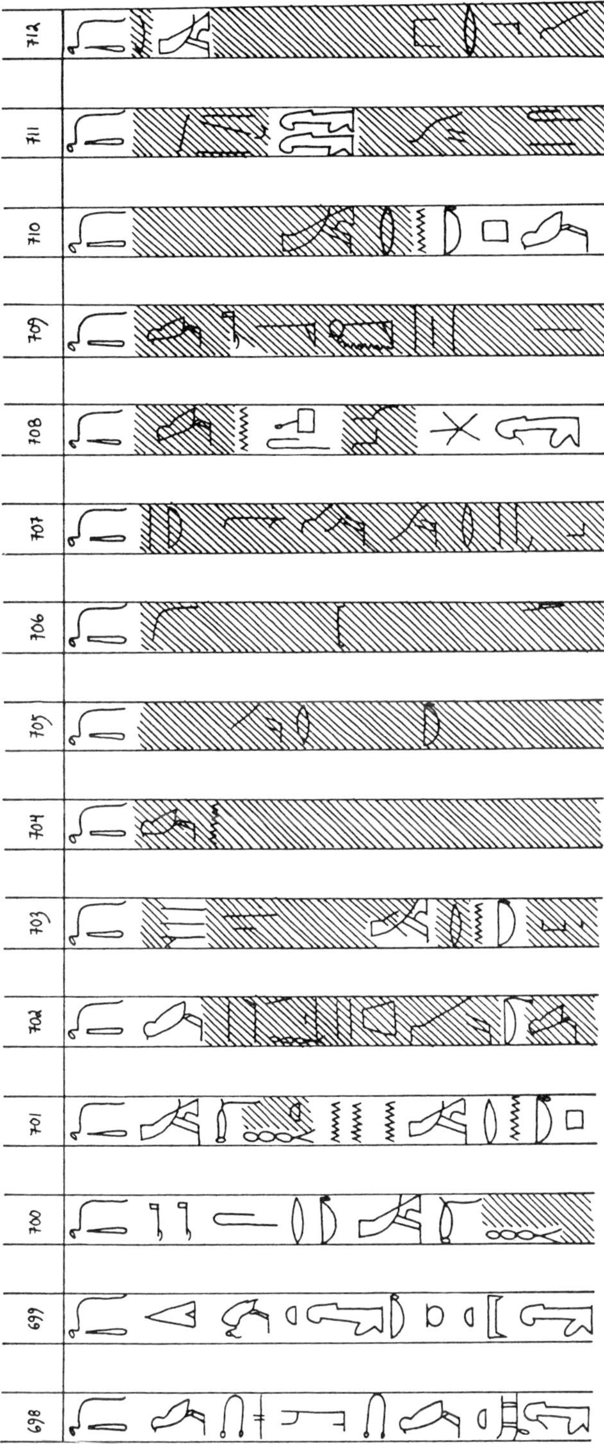

Figure 117. Hand copy, east wall, north end, Register C, lines 698–724 (continued on figure 118).

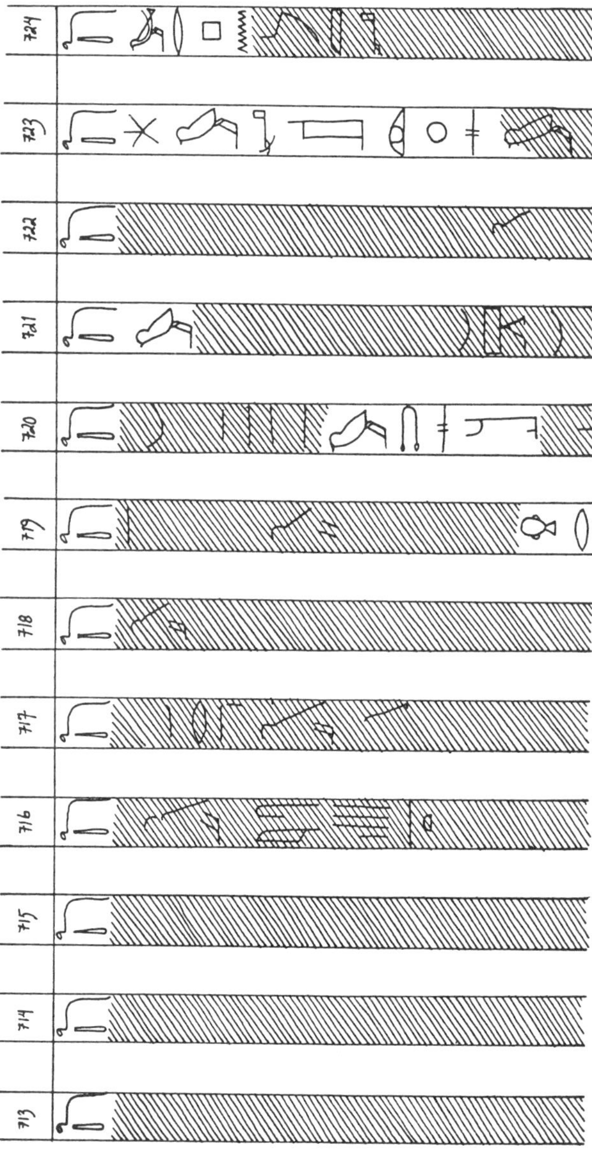

Figure 118. Hand copy, east wall, north end, Register C, lines 698–724 (continued from figure 117).

Figure 119. Hand copy, east wall, south end, Register A, lines 725–736.

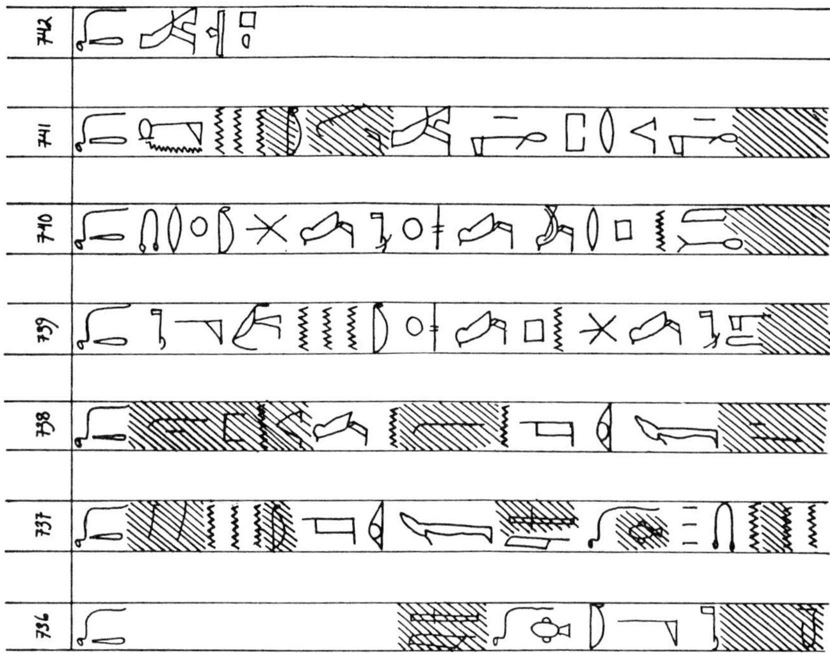

Figure 120. Hand copy, east wall, south end, Register A, lines 736–742.

Figure 121. Hand copy, east wall, south end, Register A, lines 742–752.

The Tomb Chamber of Ḥsw The Elder

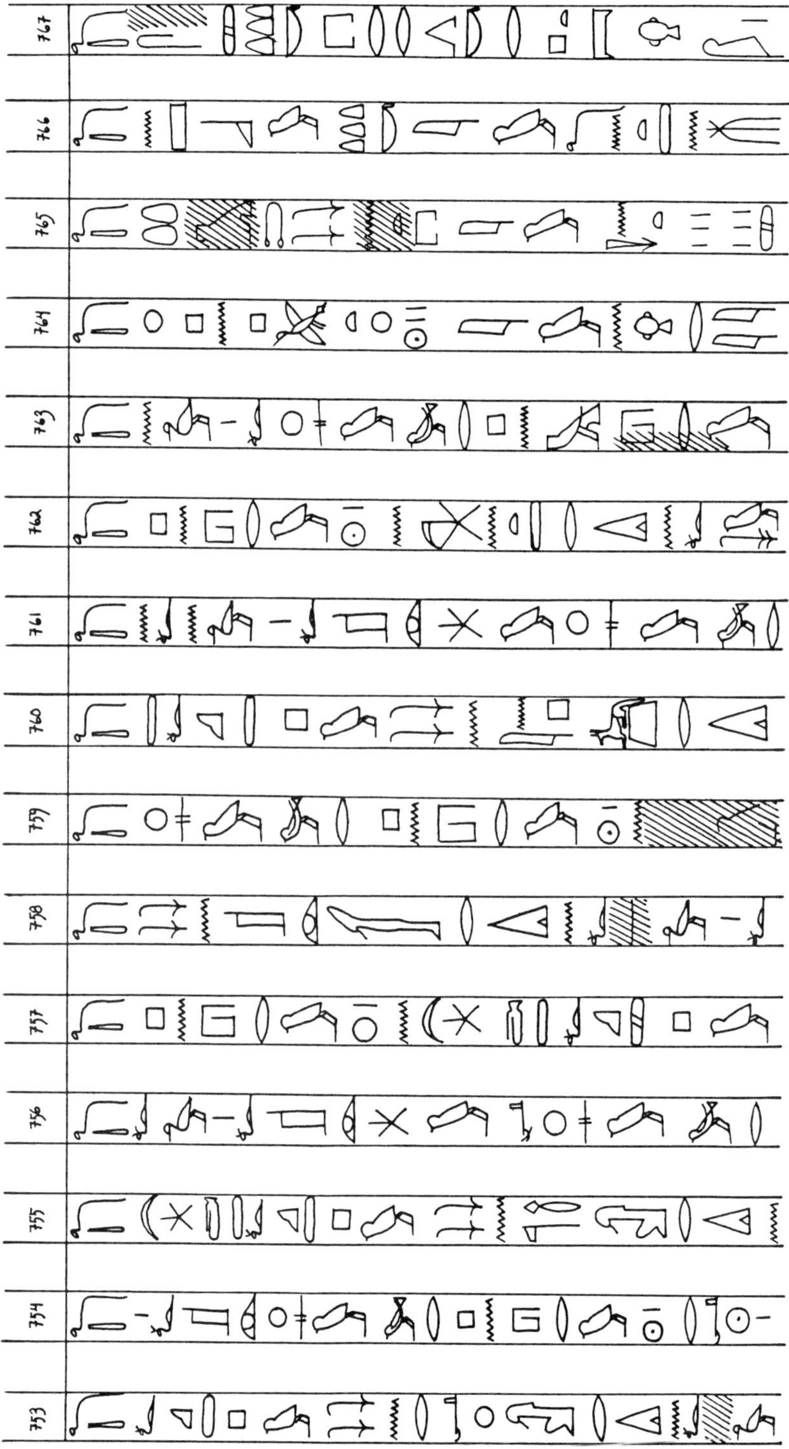

Figure 122. Hand copy, east wall, south end, Register B, lines 753–780 (continued on figure 123).

Figure 123. Hand copy, east wall, south end, Register B, lines 753–780 (continued from figure 122).

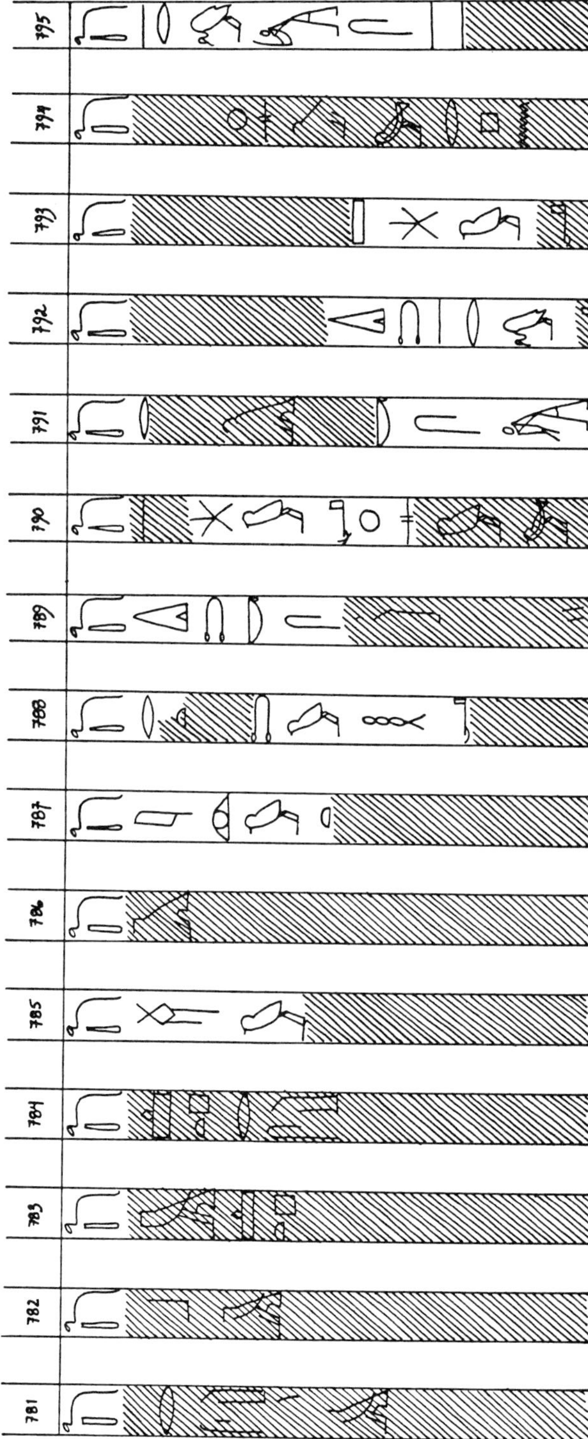

Figure 124. Hand copy, east wall, south end, Register C, lines 781–803 (continued on figure 125).

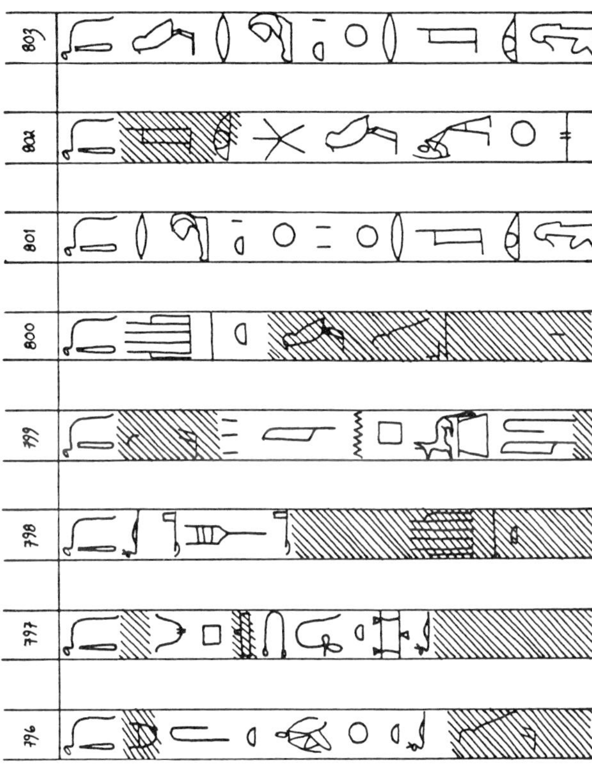

Figure 125. Hand copy, east wall, south end, Register C, lines 781–803 (continued from figure 124).

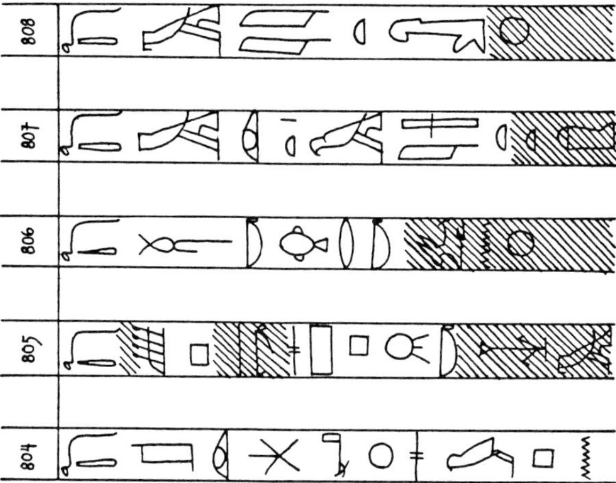

Figure 126. Hand copy, east wall, south end, Register C, lines 804–808.

Figure 127a–b. Photographs of the ceiling of the tomb.

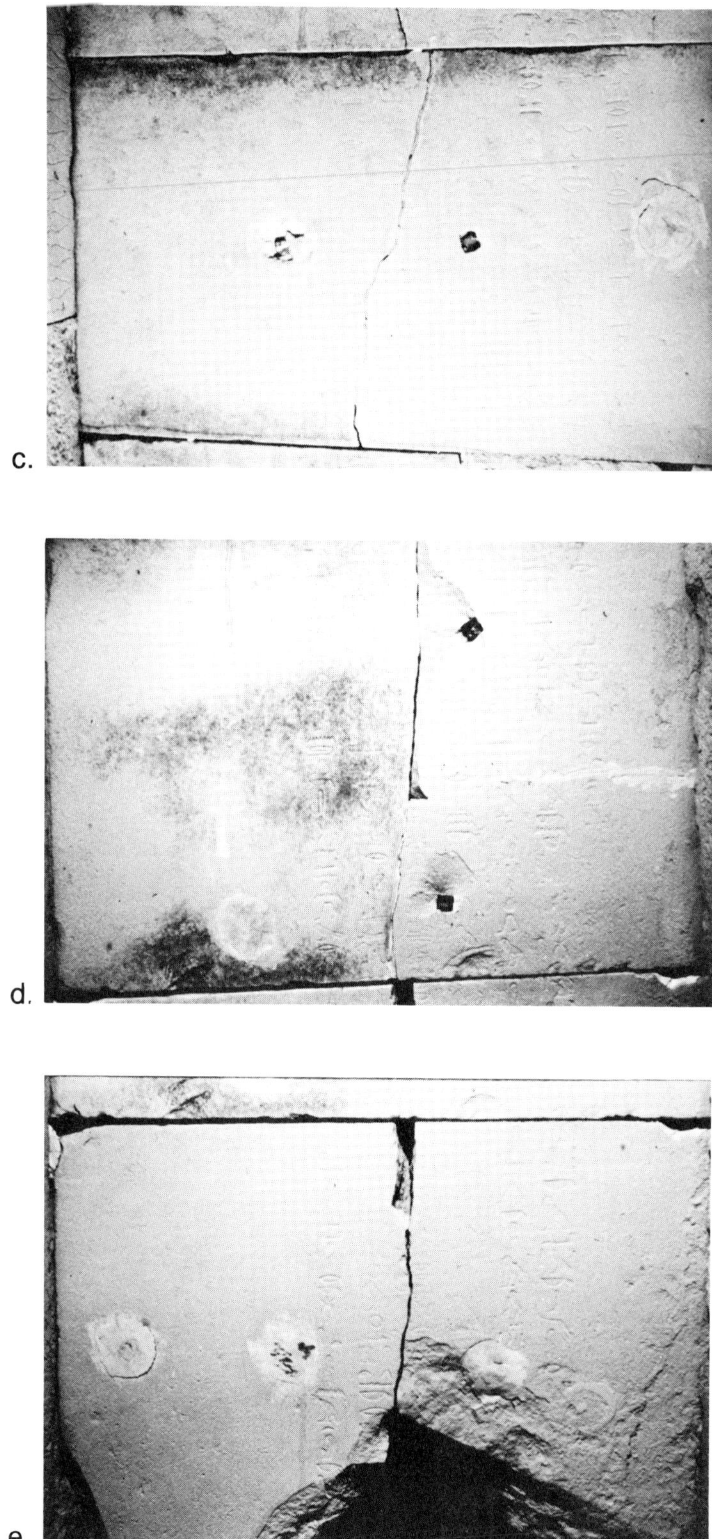

Figure 127c–e. Photographs of the ceiling of the tomb.

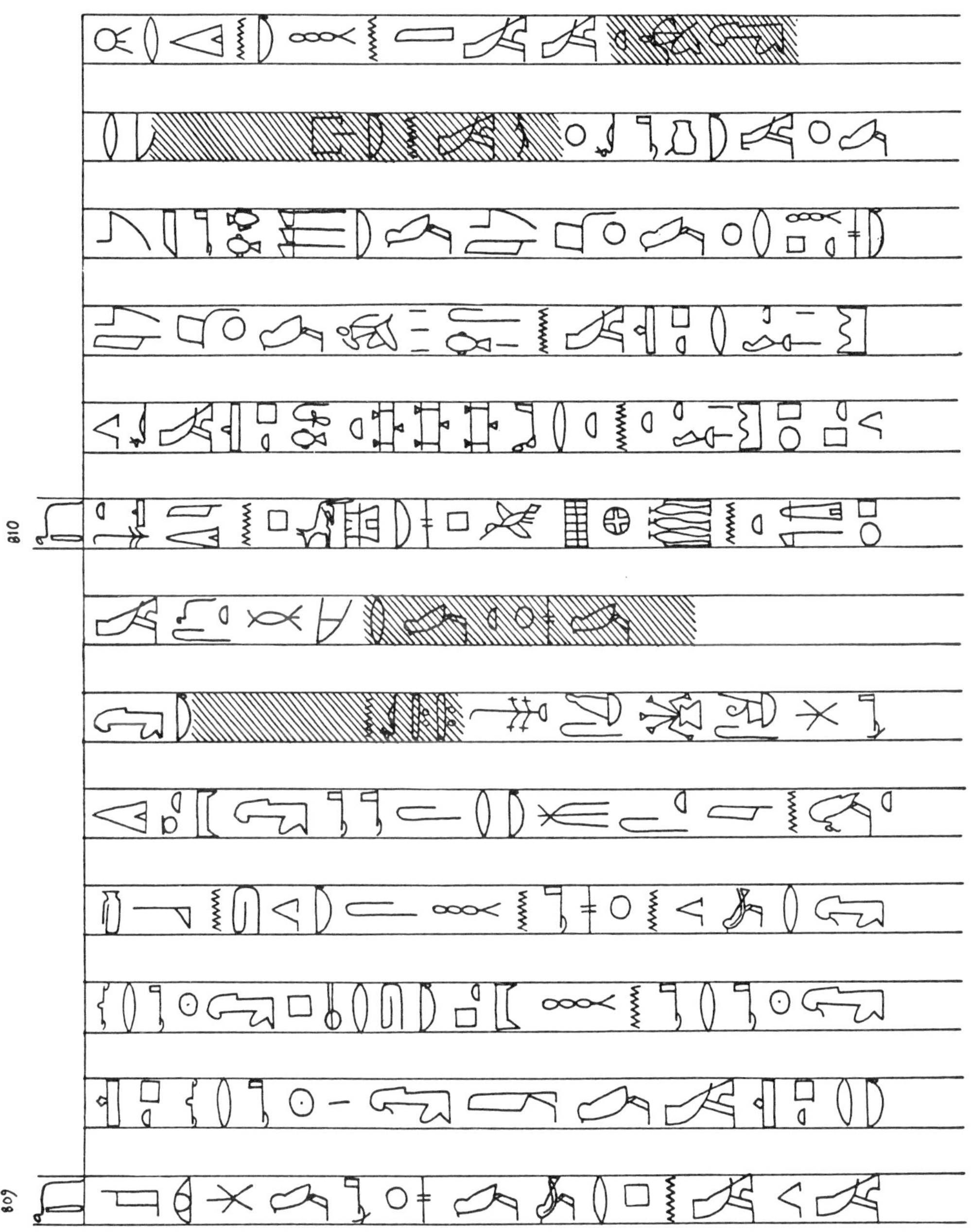

Figure 128. Hand copy, ceiling, lines 809–810.

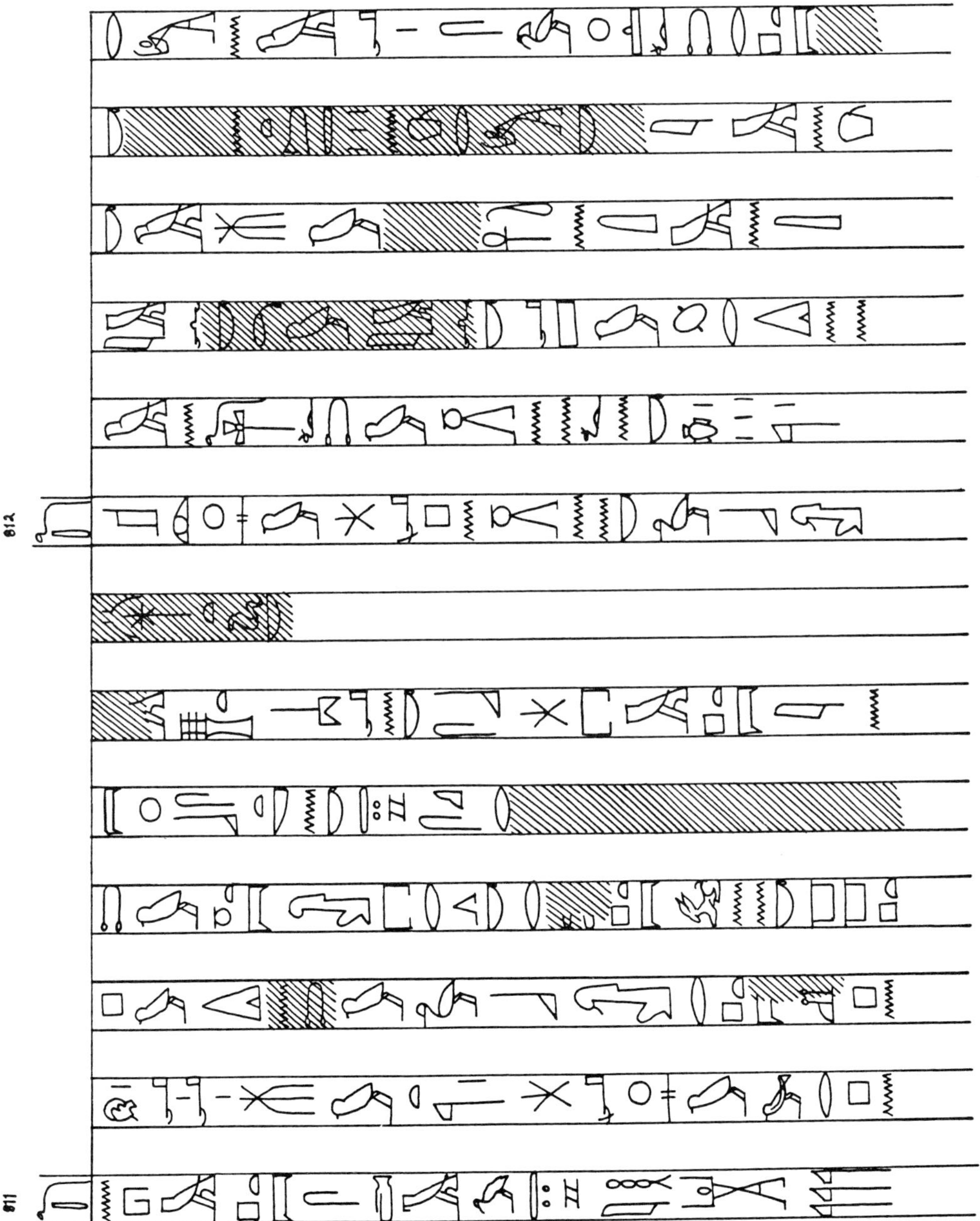

Figure 129. Hand copy, ceiling, lines 811–812.

Figure 130. Hand copy, ceiling, lines 813–814.

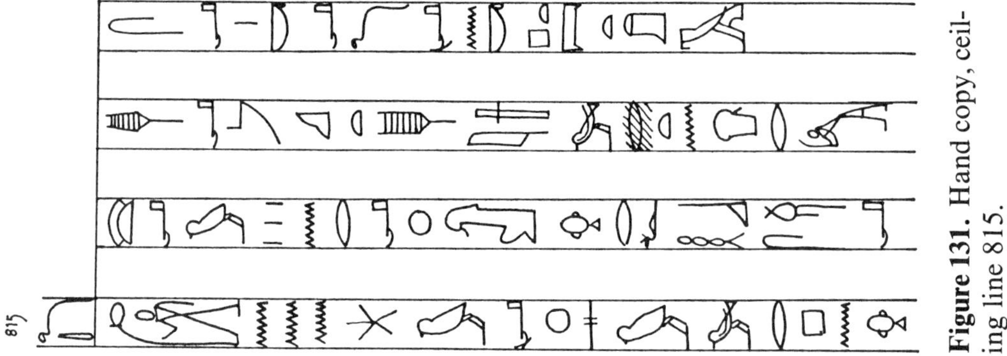

Figure 131. Hand copy, ceiling line 815.